PSYCHOBOOK

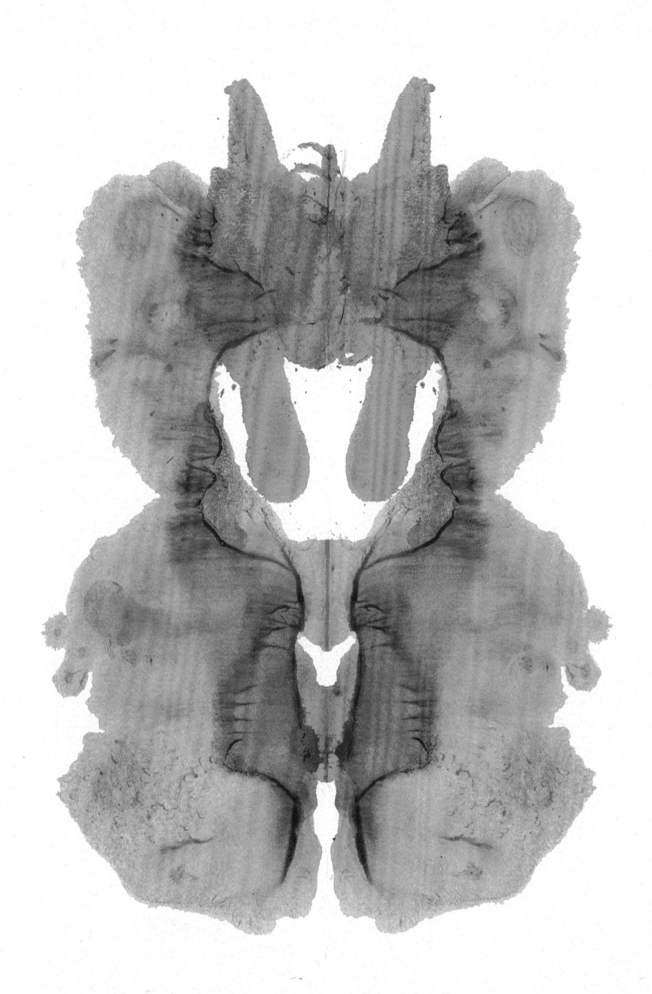

PSYCHOBOOK

EDITED BY JULIAN ROTHENSTEIN

WITH COMMENTARIES BY MEL GOODING

REDSTONE PRESS, LONDON

First published in 2016 by Redstone Press,

7a St Lawrence Terrace, London W10 5SU

www.theredstoneshop.com

978-0-9928316-2-2

A catalogue record for this book is available from the British Library

Design: Julian Rothenstein

Copy editor: Jill Hollis

Artwork: Otis Marchbank Production: Tim Chester

Manufactured by C & C Offset Printing Co. Ltd., China

Compilation © 2016 Redstone Press

Introduction © Lionel Shriver 2016

Commentaries © Mel Gooding 2016

Essay © Oisín Wall 2016

Writers Imagine Questionnaires (pages 115 to 141) © each author as credited

THANKS TO:

Neil Bartlett, Kitty Bowler, Charles Boyle, Anne Clarke, Adam Dant, Barbara Darko, Hiang Kee,
Georgia Miller, Jonathan Miller, Max Porter, Kate Pullinger, Miriam Robinson, Sophie Rochester,
Ella Rothenstein, Lucien Rothenstein, Rob Shaeffer.

PICTURE CREDITS:

Corbis: front cover, 72, 137 / British Psychological Society, History of Psychology Centre:
14, 34, 35, 41, 49, 50, 112 / Science and Society Picture Library: 22, 26, 36, 43
Redstone Press collection: 4, 20, 33, 40, 42, 44-48, 54-55, 66-70, 75-77, 99
Getty Images: 134 / © The Estate of Sigmar Polke, Cologne, DACS 2015: 179
Collection Stedelijk Museum Amsterdam: 171 / courtesy of The Kinsey Institute: 118
courtesy of The Freud Museum: 19 / courtesy of Studio Frith: 96-97
Drawings © Adam Dant: 100, 102-105, 108-111, 154-160
Photographs © Sebastian Zimmerman: 126, 132
Photographs © Nick Cunard 122, 142 / Photographs © Sarah Ainslie 79-88

Every effort has been made to contact copyright holders. Any copyright holders we have been unable to reach or to whom inaccurate acknowledgement has been made are invited to contact the publisher.

Photomontage with portraits of Sigmund Freud and Kurt Weill by Louise Dahl-Wolfe, c.1934.

CONTENTS

INTRODUCTION BY LIONEL SHRIVER

As a kid, I was always befuddled by classmates whose reigning ambition was to 'fit in' – to blend anonymously with their peers into human wallpaper. I wanted to stand out. Admittedly, I came of age in the 1960s, an era that celebrated oddity. Yet even during that age of transgressive individualism, most of my contemporaries wanted to keep their heads down. By contrast, I proudly declared that my favourite colour was black (and grew bored with people informing me that black is 'not a colour'), and that I far preferred overcast skies to sunny days (my father worried there was something wrong with my eyes). At fifteen, every day at school I wore a little black velvet tam, an unfashionable signature I was so afraid of losing that I secured it with a shoelace tucked behind my left ear and safety-pinned to my collar. A good four decades before the rest of the world followed suit, I cycled everywhere I went, refusing to learn to drive when I came of age. Using ineffectual masking tape, I decorated the ceiling of my bedroom with dangling strings of beads, which continually plopped back down on the bedspread. I strode the halls of my Atlanta high school in a homemade sash pinned with my complete political button collection – a source of great hilarity behind my back, I'm sure. I was a bit of a nutter, and I wanted to be a nutter.

Thus I've been naturally hostile to conventional psychological testing, insofar as it is designed to weed out the weirdos from the regular people. In my life, the whole concept of the normal has functioned as a neutral backdrop against which I can loom forward in relief. Of course, throughout my adulthood, the drive to slot everyone into a category, to slap a diagnosis on every variation from the mean, has only accelerated. Indeed, we now live in a time when if you don't have a diagnosis you don't know who you are, and people wave their designated psychiatric ailments like football trophies. With a wealth of new classifications at our disposal, we can easily peg me now: I am an attention seeker. Damn straight. I have sought attention and often got it, if not always the nice kind.

Granted, in adulthood I have repudiated the careless view popular in the 1960s that it's the crazy people who are sane, and the sane are crazy. There's such as thing a crazy, and it isn't pretty; serious mental illness rarely entails access to a higher truth. But then, serious mental illness isn't subtle, either, and therapists contending with a raving schizophrenic don't generally need to resort to questionnaires.

As a novelist, too, I instinctively resist the quantification of character, the reduction of such an elusive concept to a set of measurements, to a score. Theoretically, I suppose, fiction writers might construct protagonists by choosing numerical points on various key continuums: on a scale of one to ten, say, our hero scores two for 'fearfulness', nine for 'openness to new experience', one for 'risk aversion', eight for 'ego strength'. . . But good luck with charting out our story's principals in this manner and coming up with Pierre in *War and Peace*. In other words, even when they are not misleading, the results of much psychiatric testing is crudely descriptive, and tell you little you didn't know before.

Nevertheless, the psychological tests collected in this book are often compelling, if only, especially in the early, more historical instances, compellingly stupid. Some of the statements are comical: 'I do not like to see men in their pyjamas.' Some of the questions invite wistful existential speculation: if asked, 'Does the future seem pointless?' who wouldn't, on some days, say 'yes'? Ditto, 'Do you feel that there is some sort of barrier between you and other people so that you can't really understand them?' Isn't that the standard state of affairs between anybody and anybody? Isn't real intimacy the exception? And the few folks who fail to confess, 'I do not always tell the truth', are lying, if only to themselves.

Psycho-quizzes are also blind to context – the specific circumstances that dictate even truthful answers to which the test is oblivious. An air traffic controller might agree, 'I work under a great deal of tension' without having an anxiety disorder. A Nobel laureate might affirm 'I am an important person' without being a narcissist. A well-adjusted subject who concurs 'It would be better if almost all laws were thrown away' obviously lives in the EU. A woman who concedes 'Once a week or oftener I feel suddenly hot all over without apparent cause' may simply be over fifty. These days, those who tick a box beside 'Are people talking about you and criticizing you through no fault of your own?' aren't implicitly paranoid; they participate in social media. Likewise, a tick next to 'Someone has been trying to get into my car' means something different depending on the neighbourhood where the car has been parked. Were I to check, 'Once in a while I think of things too bad to talk about', it would help the test-giver to know that I write novels and thinking abominations is my job.

What's especially stupid about much psychological testing is that the psychologists think we're stupid. That is, the test designers fail to give subjects credit for being able to intuit the purpose of the test, and thus which answers it is in their interest to provide. Even way-back-when, looking at Rorschach inkblots, half-sussed patients knew perfectly well that they were better off seeing not bats but butterflies. Were you to tick, when taking a personality test as part of a job application, 'I am afraid I am going out of my mind', you would indeed be out of your mind. One is reminded of those naff American visa applications that ask, 'Are you a terrorist?' And then when jihadists manage to slip through this brutal interrogation anyway, law enforcement is consternated.

In a circular fashion, even the later, more playful tests in this book rely on self-knowledge to generate self-knowledge. When taking 'The Family Relationship Test' (a set of drawings from which to pick the best pictorial representation of you and your kin), subjects who select image #4 – three figures looking passively on while one figure lugs loads of baggage – know full well they feel imposed upon by relatives without looking up the key at the back ('burdened') or they wouldn't have chosen that answer. As an expat who has put the Atlantic Ocean between herself and her family, I had no trouble selecting image #5: three figures in the foreground bent towards one another, while a smaller figure in the distance runs away. But then, I already knew I was an absconder ('escaping', according to the key), which is why I circled #5 in the first place. What have we accomplished? (Though the drawings are charming.)

In other instances, there may be a big difference between what subjects claim they would do in a given hypothetical situation, and what they would really do. For example, in the 'Matter in the Wrong Place' Test, I answered the theoretical 'Your partner adopts the annoying habit of turning on the kettle most times they walk past it' with c) 'You politely explain to your partner that there is little advantage in keeping water close to boiling point in this way.' But anyone (like my husband) horribly familiar with my bossy, autocratic *modus operandi* in the home would have chosen d) 'You seek to impose a ban, to nip this insidious habit in the bud. It could lead to other bad habits, after all.'

Yet if you usually know the answers – anyone who lives in an unabating state of rage probably doesn't need a questionnaire to identify an 'angry' temperament – why are these tests so addictive? In general, the earlier examples in this book are efforts by authorities to identify aberrant proclivities for their own evil purposes, whereas the more recent, more open-ended tests in the latter chapters encourage self-exploration, but taking both types is entertaining. Once freed from the anxiety about failure that school days impose on the experience, test taking is fun; it's a game. Psychological tests are an opportunity to look in the mirror, and recognizing traits in ourselves is validating, regardless of which traits they are. Personally, I'm more apt to look for evidence that I'm an outlier rather than for proof that I'm just like everybody else, an inclination that lately, alas, makes me just like everybody else: while Western culture grows more conformist politically, in respect to sex and psychology we have grown less normative. As an alternative to an amorphous blob, any form reflected back at us is a relief: *I am fucked up, therefore I am*. It was curiously satisfying to take The Shyness Questionnaire and confirm that I am far shyer than most friends would imagine, even if I knew that already.

Psychobook is part comedy, part history, part self-help, and part coffee-table *objet d'art*. It's part sincere, part tongue-in-cheek, part meditation, part mockery, but its production is universally beautiful, its sensibility universally droll. I suggest reading it with a pencil.

MENTAL MEDDLERS:
A BRIEF HISTORY OF PSYCHOLOGICAL TESTING
OISÍN WALL

Psychological testing has always been an expression of power – from the colonial assumptions of nineteenth-century anthropometrists to the pastoral power of the psychologist today. Psychological testers agree on a normal range of emotions, behaviours, intelligence, etc. and by doing so they identify people outside this range as abnormal or deviant. Over the last century people have exploited this power to discriminate against, lock up, and even sterilise their fellow human beings.

Psychological testing has also been an expression of hope: from the Soviet Union to the United States of America psychological tests have been hailed by many as a way to achieve a fairer society. Generations of psychologists have worked tirelessly to improve the tests, to overcome biases, and to use them to enable people to overcome class and social disadvantages.

Many writers like to claim that psychological testing has ancient roots and, depending on the point they are trying to make or the audience they are trying to court, they point to sources from the Bible to the Chinese civil service in the second millennium BCE. However, the first major practice which claimed to objectively and scientifically measure a psychological trait was craniometry. It emerged in the eighteenth century and claimed that by measuring the skull it was possible to discover the size of the brain and, by extension, the extent of a person's intelligence. In the late eighteenth century this was refined into phrenology, which claimed that the shape of the skull could be used to map which 'organs' of the brain were better developed. The assumption was that these organs could be mapped, in turn, onto psychological characteristics such as language, parental love, self-esteem and musicality.

Through the growing interest in phrenology we can see the emergence of a trend that has dogged psychological testing throughout its history. As early as 1821 Johann Gaspar Spurzheim, a leading phrenologist in Britain and France, argued that, through phrenology, hereditary tendencies towards criminality could be identified and therefore bred out of society. In time a clear pattern began to emerge in phrenological literature. White middle-class men from northern Europe, with a few notable exceptions, had the best heads – they showed strength of character and intelligence – while everyone else, from the European working class to colonized Africans, had skulls that told of intemperance, violence, and stupidity. Ireland had proved to be a troublesome colony throughout the nineteenth century, and Irish skulls came in for particular criticism. George Combe, a leading British phrenologist, declared, based on his phrenological study, that Irish Catholics were 'coarse, grovelling, and unintellectual'. But he reassured his readership, who were no doubt worried by ongoing Catholic emancipation, that these very traits meant that Ireland would never have the wherewithal to challenge the racially superior authority of Britain. Inevitably political narratives were played out through phrenology. The right of the wealthy to rule the poor and the right of the European empires to rule the world were buttressed by this pseudo-science.

As interest in phrenology declined, new psychological tests began to emerge. The first that relied on the test-subject to actually respond to stimuli, rather than simply being poked, prodded and measured, emerged in anthropometry in the late nineteenth century. One of the most vocal proponents of these tests was Francis Galton, an anthropologist and statistician who invented the dog whistle, established the whorl-loop-arch approach to analysing fingerprints, and coined the term eugenics. In 1884 Galton established an 'anthropometric laboratory' at the South Kensington Museum's Health Exhibition, the precursor in London to today's Science Museum. If members of the public paid three shillings, Galton would measure everything that he could think of from breathing capacity to reaction times. He built up a lot of interest in psychological testing but was acutely aware that he was failing to measure the 'keenness of the senses'. By the time the lab closed in the 1890s it had measured over nine thousand people, and similar labs had been opened around the world, bringing with them psychological tests, dog whistles, and eugenics.

In 1904 Alfred Binet, a self-taught psychologist, was tasked by the French Minister of Public Education with identifying schoolchildren who were having difficulties academically. Binet devised a series of tasks which were assessed and marked to give a single score called the pupil's 'mental age'. If this was below their chronological age they received special education. While Binet's test assessed educational development, William Stern, a German psychologist, claimed that the same test could be used to measure intelligence itself. He developed the idea of 'mental age' into an 'intelligence quotient' (IQ) by calculating that IQ was the ratio of mental age to chronological age times one hundred.

During the First World War psychological testing was viewed rather sceptically in Europe, but things were different in the United States of America. Before the war, in 1908, Henry H. Goddard had interpreted Binet's work for America, introducing a strict new marking system and the terms 'moron' and 'feeble-minded' to describe ranges of abnormally low 'mental age' and IQ scores. Although the army was nervous of the 'mental meddlers', as one general referred to them, between 1918 and 1919 Robert M. Yerkes and the other American military psychologists used tests based on Goddard's work to evaluate more than 1.1 million men.

Like phrenology and anthropometric testing before it, intelligence testing tended to find that the children of wealthy white parents were more intelligent than everyone else. What was different, however, was that intelligence testing had a direct influence on American lawmakers, fuelling a campaign of legal, as well as social and cultural, discrimination. In 1912 Goddard had recommended that anyone classified as 'feeble-minded' should be segregated and stopped from having children; others went further. By the end of the First World War, fifteen American States had passed compulsory eugenic sterilisation laws and by 1937 that number had risen to thirty-three. Ultimately, between 1907 and 1970, around sixty thousand 'mental defectives' were sterilised in America. In the 1920s and 1930s similar laws were enacted on this side of the Atlantic, from Denmark to Switzerland, and, of course, in Germany in 1933.

This eugenic movement was greatly encouraged by the American army's wartime psychological testing. The tests claimed to measure innate intelligence but were written by white middle-class men and relied on cultural signifiers that those men regarded as obvious. As you might expect, groups who were not familiar with the signifiers, like immigrants, often did poorly in these tests. In 1912 Goddard was invited to conduct tests of new immigrants on Ellis Island and concluded that 'the test results established that 83% of the Jews, 80% of the Hungarians, 79% of the Italians and 87% of the Russians were "feeble-minded" '.[1] A few years later an American analysis of the army intelligence tests made the story that the tests told more explicit: 'at one extreme we have the distribution of the Nordic race group. At the other extreme we have the American negro'. But the tests did not only pick out people of different ethnic or racial backgrounds. The American working class appeared to be intellectual infants. Industrial and agricultural workers made up the majority of the 1.1 million recruits and draftees tested during the First World War, and the tests concluded that the average mental age of a white American man was about thirteen years old; it was lower still for black soldiers. While this prompted some to question whether the mental age scale was really as accurate as they thought, others, like William McDougall, a professor of psychology at Harvard University, pointedly asked 'is America safe for democracy?' Nor was this kind of 'scientific' racism limited to America, a British study in 1925 produced similar results. Margaret Moul and Karl Pearson, Francis Galton's protégé, claimed that more than 57% of Russian and Polish Jewish immigrant children could be classed as 'slow', 'dull', 'very dull' or 'mentally defective.' Based on their results Pearson and Moul asked: 'What purpose would there be in endeavouring to legislate for a superior breed of men, if at any moment it could be swamped by the influx of immigrants of an inferior race, hastening to profit by the higher civilisation of an improved humanity?'[2]

By the early 1920s, psychological tests were gathering support in Europe. Influential psychologists, like Charles Samuel Myers who had published the first paper on 'shellshock' in 1915, were pushing hard to expand the social role of psychological testing. Through institutions like the National Institute of Industrial Psychology, they advised companies on how they could test potential employees and schools on how to test students. Schools and teachers around the world jumped at the possibility of using standardised tests to assess students' natural abilities. For some it seemed that this was a chance to level the playing field between rich and poor, while others hoped that it would be a scientific justification for maintaining national, racial and class divisions.

This new wave of enthusiasm, however, carried with it more than IQ tests. After the success of the Woodworth Personal Data Sheet (PDS) in America during the War, the 1920s and 1930s saw a flourishing of personality tests. These tests became increasingly sophisticated in the 1920s. In 1919 the PDS asked questions like 'Did you ever think that you had lost your manhood?' and innocently expected subjects to understand the idiom and to answer honestly. Later tests developed a more critical approach to asking questions and cross-referencing answers. Over the next few decades thousands of different personality tests hit the market. Some were long and tedious lists of questions. Others, like the Lowenfeld Mosaic test, allowed subjects to construct images or scenarios through which emotions and ideas could be expressed. Still others were 'projective', presenting the subject with images or other stimuli and allowing them to 'project' their own meaning; perhaps the most famous of these is the Rorschach 'inkblot' test, developed in 1921.

[1] Leon J. Kamin, *The Science and Politics of IQ*, Routledge, (London, 1974), page 16

[2] Karl Pearson and Margaret Moul, 'The Problem of Alien Immigration into Great Britain, illustrated by an Examination of Russian and Polish Jewish Children', *Annals of Eugenics*, Vol. 1, Issue 1, page 16. Blackwell Publishing Ltd. / University College, London, 1925

Also in 1921, Carl Jung, Freud's prodigal protégé, opened a new debate when he published *Psychological Types*. He popularised the idea that it was possible to identify which psychological function was dominant – sensation, intuition, thinking, or feeling – and, by combining that with whether the person was an introvert or extrovert, to decide what 'type' the person was. Jung's idea set something of a trend and, over the following century, countless psychologists attempted to establish the basic personality types: some identified thousands, others suggested that there were as few as five. However, without consensus on a working model, personality testing did not become as culturally widespread as other forms of psychological tests. However it did make major inroads into the world of clinical psychology where personality tests, and particularly projective tests, were found to be diagnostically and therapeutically useful.

The 1920s and early 1930s were, perhaps, the most optimistic period in the history of psychological testing. Many prominent researchers believed that tests could be used to reform or even revolutionise society. If, they argued, people's intelligence, rather than their education, could be tested, then poor but intelligent people could be advanced to positions of power, instead of stupid wealthy people. At that time this idea was particularly strong in the Soviet Union, where some psychologists hoped that tests could be used to create the proletarian culture and the 'new man' that they believed would emerge in post-revolutionary society. In other countries, like the USA, psychologists argued that crime and poverty could be drastically reduced by identifying and addressing the needs of people with learning difficulties, or intelligent people who were being held back by their environment. In Britain intelligence testing was championed by left-wing educationalists like R. H. Tawney, who saw it as a challenge to the privileged position of the aristocracy and the public-school-educated bourgeoisie. Like the Soviets, many on the British left argued that testing would allow for the rational planning of a society based on the skills of the people.

As you might have guessed, the optimism regarding psychological testing as a great leveller did not last. Just as in the West, many of the tests in the Soviet Union found that the working class, the peasantry and national minorities tended not to do so well as urban, educated, former bourgeoisie. Believing that even communist psychologists were biased by their bourgeois backgrounds and training, in 1936 psychological testing of children was banned across the Soviet Union. For similar reasons in Britain, many groups that had advocated its egalitarian power also began to turn against psychological testing in the late 1930s. Around the same time in France, many schools began to reject the Binet tests either for their perceived bias or because they were seen to usurp the role of teachers in the classroom.

The Second World War gave psychological testing another chance to shine. Building on the advances of industrial and vocational testing in the inter-war years, psychological testing was set to work on the war machine. It was used to assess and allocate specific roles to soldiers, sailors and airmen according to their skills, intelligence and personality traits. Intelligence testing was widely used, but because Germany had soured, to say the least, the idea of eugenics for most people, no grand discriminatory decisions were taken based on the tests, as they had been in the aftermath of the previous war.

After the war, the rate at which new psychological tests were being produced slowed, although they continued to grow in popularity. Even though most people, as already mentioned, turned away from the eugenic and racist side of psychological testing after the shock of the liberation of the concentration camps, there were a few who never fully disentangled themselves. In the late 1960s a number of influential scientists in Britain and America published books and articles supporting the view that black people, among others, had genetically lower IQs. In 1972 William Shockley, a Nobel laureate, even proposed a 'sterilisation bonus plan'. Under this plan people who voluntarily submitted to sterilisation would receive $1,000 for every IQ point less than 100 that they scored. Nor was Shockley alone in this idea. Many prominent scientists, particularly in North America, have been and continue to be funded by groups like The Pioneer Fund to promote ideas about eugenics and heredity.

Psychological tests had come under attack from some quarters as early as the 1930s and this intensified in the 1960s and 1970s as racial interpretation of IQ tests again began to gain in popularity. People attacked everything from the underlying ideology of the new racial studies to the reliability of psychological testing in general, and even its foundational principles. A particularly serious blow came in the mid 1970s when a string of articles and books began to dismantle the legacy of Cyril Burt, an influential British educational psychologist knighted for his contribution to psychology, a former president of the British Psychological Association, and Galton Professor of Eugenics at University College London. They claimed that Burt, who had been a leading proponent of the idea that intelligence was inherited, had misinterpreted important data, falsified many of his results, and even invented imaginary collaborators. The 'Burt affair' cast a shadow over the entire field of intelligence testing. Personality tests also came under fire from several influential books arguing that behaviour is socially and environmentally shaped and so cannot be predicted by a set of tests conducted in controlled circumstances.

In spite of these attacks, psychological testing had become more common than ever by the mid-1980s. Around this time the 'Big Five' consensus emerged. Many psychologists agreed that there were five basic personality factors: Extraversion, Agreeableness, Conscientiousness, Emotional Stability and Openness to Experience. This provided a working model for personality testing, and the 1990s and 2000s saw the personality test gain new levels of acceptance both clinically and in vocational assessments. Today psychological tests are an everyday phenomenon. We encounter them in school, university, job interviews and in clinics. Not to mention the countless pseudo-psychological tests that we see daily in magazines, on the internet and on social media, which collect data for advertising agencies and others while promising to tell us which celebrity we are most like, what animal we are, or who we should vote for.

For most of us psychological testing today seems neither threatening nor hopeful, but simply another part of the constant measuring and comparing that fills modern life. The power and the optimism of psychological testing, however, lie in the statistical correlation of results, the comparison of hundreds or thousands of test scores. Without this correlation psychological tests have no power to discriminate between normal and deviant, but they do allow us to probe ourselves and our assumptions about others.

Sigmund Freud, c.1920. Photographer unknown.

Doodles classified: diagnostic chart from *Major Types of Graphomotor Protocols*, USA, 1950s.

1

CLASSIC PSYCHOLOGICAL TESTS

Non-linguistic intelligence tests developed in the 1920s and involving exercises in
sequencing, matching, patterning, and logical connection.

Intelligence testing at Ellis Island, USA, c.1910. Pioneered by Howard
Andrew Knox, these tests, which used graphic puzzles similar to those
shown opposite, were intended to determine the mental capacity of
potential immigrants.

LOWENFELD MOSAIC TESTS

The box contains 465 wooden pieces in six colours and eight geometric shapes (squares, diamonds and three types of triangle – right angle, isosceles, and scalene). It was intended for use with children, but some psychologists have extended its use to adult patients. Test subjects were invited to make any pattern or image they liked. The analysis of outcomes was related to the subject's behaviour during the tests (e.g. whether anxious or carefree, determined or haphazard, thoughtful or careless, etc.) and/or the patterns produced (whether ordered or random, figurative or abstract, etc.) The tests, introduced by the respected British child psychologist Margaret Lowenfeld in 1929, are still in use today.

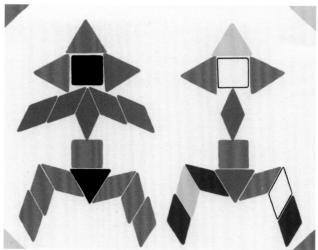

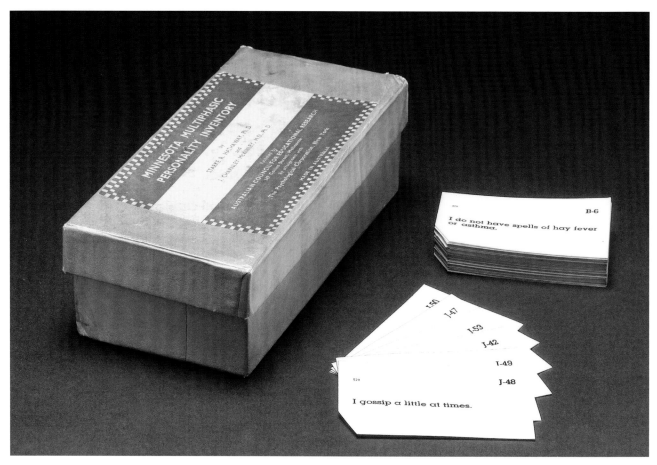

Box and numbered inventory cards for the MMPI.

MINNESOTA MULTIPHASIC PERSONALITY INVENTORY (MMPI)

The University of Minnesota Press first published the MMPI in 1943. The statements that appear on pages 27 to 29 are similar to those used in the MMPI and other psychometric tests developed as aids to personality analysis and to the diagnosis of psychological and psychopathological conditions. These tests, or developments of them, continue to be widely used by clinical psychologists. They are designed to reveal traits and predispositions that may be regarded as 'normal' or 'deviant' (depression, paranoia, etc.), according to the definitions of those terms at any time in vogue with the profession. The subject is required to respond simply and without elaboration: 'yes', 'no', 'true', 'false', or 'cannot say'. Such limited responses are regarded as enabling a high degree of standardisation, producing 'objective tests' as opposed to so-called 'projective tests', which require more interpretation.

I am not afraid of toads

My father could be described as dominating

People who do not know me hesitate before shaking my hand

I am sometimes fearful without any particular reason

People who are jealous of me have hindered my career

I am not afraid of going to my doctor

My parents' marriage was very happy

I do not like to see men in their pyjamas

I do not want to be better looking

Sometimes I feel very happy for no good reason

I get over-excited when I gamble

I am not afraid of contracting infectious diseases

I do not like to hear strangers singing

Someone has been trying to get into my car

My hands have not become clumsy or awkward

I am afraid I am going out of my mind

I have a good appetite

I wake up fresh and rested most mornings

I think I would like the work of a librarian

I am easily awakened by noise

My hands and feet are usually warm enough

There seems to be a lump in my throat much of the time

I work under a great deal of tension

Once in a while I think of things too bad to talk about

My father is a good man

My mother is a good woman

My sex life is satisfactory

At times I have very much wanted to leave home

I see things or animals or people around me that others do not see

I hardly ever feel pain in the back of the neck

I am an important person

I have had periods of days, weeks, or months when I couldn't take care of things because I couldn't 'get going'

I do not always tell the truth

My judgment is better than it ever was

Once a week or oftener I feel suddenly hot all over without apparent cause

It would be better if almost all laws were thrown away

My soul sometimes leaves my body

I am in just as good physical health as most of my friends

I prefer to pass by school friends, or people I know but have not seen for a long time, unless they speak to me first

I am liked by most people who know me

I have not lived the right kind of life

Parts of my body often have feelings like burning, tingling, or crawling

I am sometimes paralyzed by fear

Sometimes I know in advance I am going to act like a fool

I often feel guilty at the same time as feeling blameless

THE SZONDI TEST

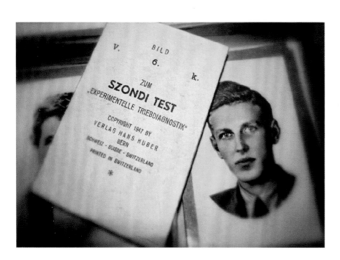

Invented by the Hungarian psychiatrist, Léopold Szondi, in 1935, this highly dubious test is based on the reactions of patients to six sets of photographic portraits of mental patients or 'psychopaths', each set containing pictures of eight psychotic personality types: homosexual, sadist, epileptic, hysteric, catatonic, paranoid, depressive and maniac! Given the absurdity of these classifications, no more need be said about the test, itself based on an elaborate and utterly ridiculous theory of elective fate.

The sinister-looking Szondi Test kit, with cards and analytic table. If your psychotherapist turns up with one of these, make an excuse and leave.

31

THE ODOR IMAGINATION TEST

In this test a blindfolded subject is given the following instructions:

I am going to let you smell various odors. As I present each of them to you I want you to invent a short anecdote or episode suggested by the odor. Please try to develop your story from the first association that comes to mind.

The following odors might be presented:

ginger, sage, soap and water, acetone, tobacco, art gum eraser, violet perfume, whiskey, sulphonaphthol, Worcestershire sauce, pine, spearmint, denatured alcohol, vinegar, germicide, sweet starch, benzoine, asafoetida, carbon tetrachloride, hydrogen sulphide gas, after-shave lotion, shellac, salad oil, sour milk, and oil of cloves.

No results of the use of this test have been published.

From Bernard I. Murstein, *The Handbook of Projective Techniques*, (Basic Books), USA, 1965.

THE FACES TEST

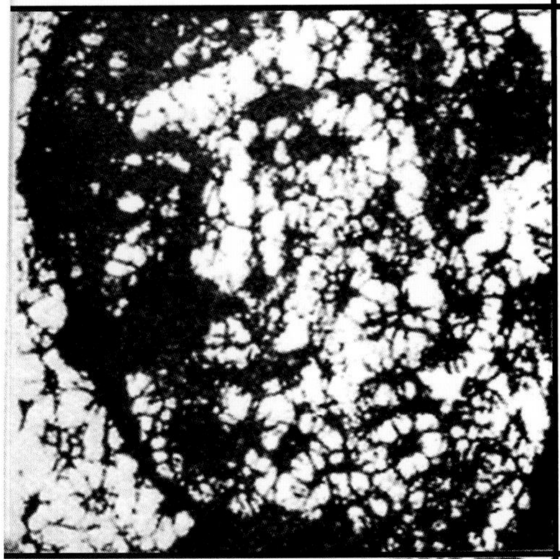

1

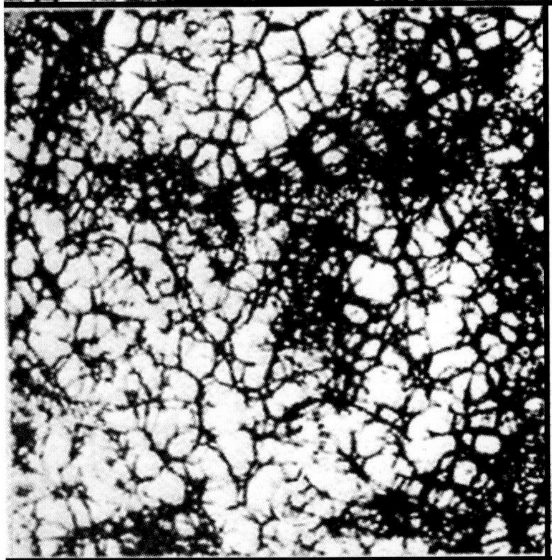

2

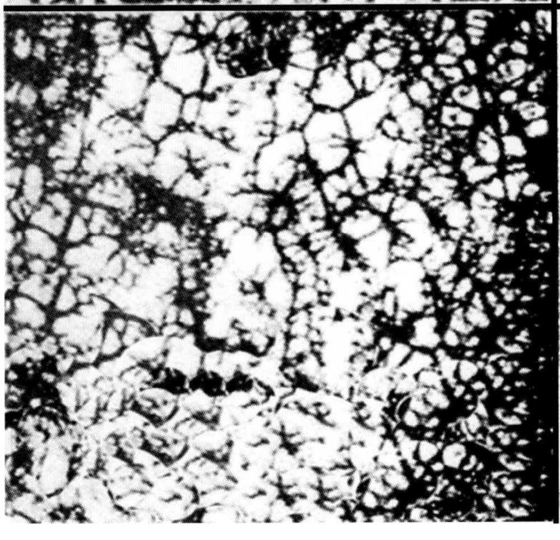

3

The subject is asked to describe the character of the person depicted. The vagueness of the image is intended to induce perceptual concentration while providing minimal visual information. Imaginative projection is thereby intensified.

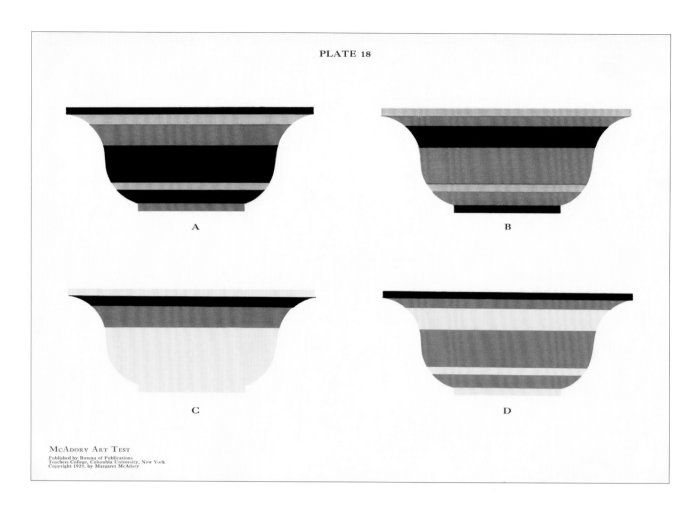

THE McADORY ART TEST

The McAdory Art Test, devised by Margaret McAdory in 1933, is one of a number of tests that purport to aid assessment of aesthetic sensitivity or artistic taste as measurable psychological predispositions, or to reveal 'artistic aptitudes'. Which is the best design? Any such judgment is both necessarily subjective and culturally determined. Taste is convention; aptitude is given but conditioned. Change is possible in both categories. It's fun, though: which do you think is the best design?

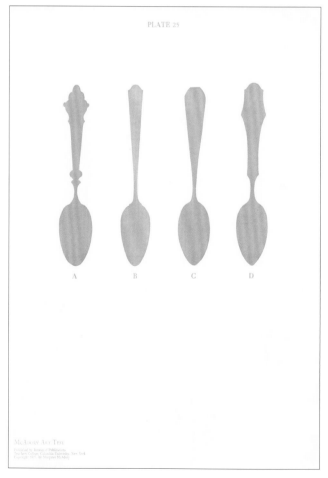

PLATE 34

A

B

C

D

McADORY ART TEST

Published by Bureau of Publications
Teachers College, Columbia University, New York
Copyright 1929, by Margaret McAdory

Bold play-blocks designed in the early twentieth century to test a child's ability to match, sequence, or make logical patterns.

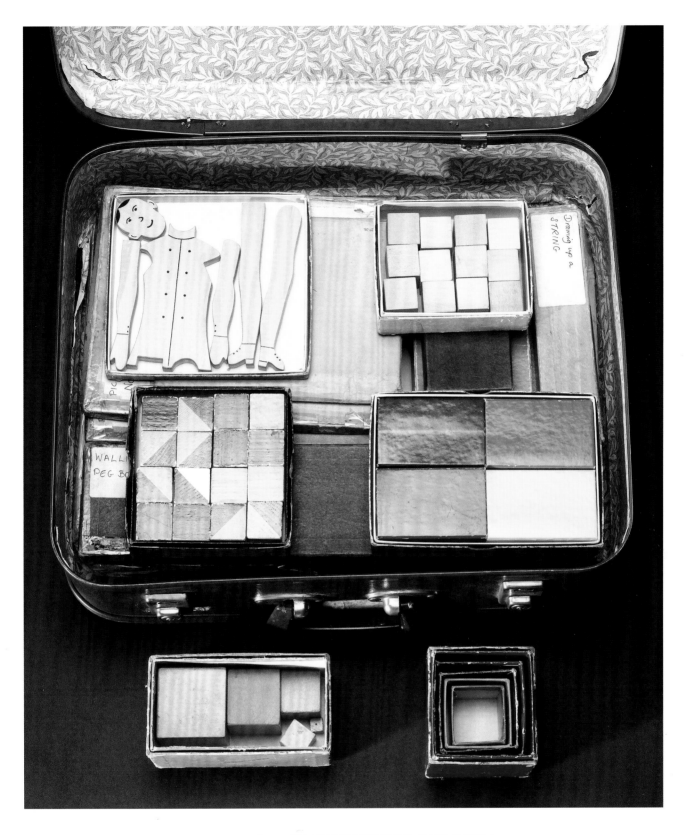

PSYCHOLOGICAL AND INTELLIGENCE TEST KIT FOR CHILDREN

In the early twentieth century, peripatetic paediatricians carried this handy little suitcase of test equipment from school to school. It contains play-blocks, building bricks of various sizes and shapes, concentric box tests, etc. It is a touching reminder of the radically changing ideas at that period: ideas about how children learn, and how they might express themselves in test situations. Intelligence was becoming recognised as the exercise of the mind, rather than as the mechanical ability to repeat what is taught by rote.

MAKE A PICTURE STORY TEST (MAPS)

Invented by American psychologist E. S. Shneidman in 1942, the test requires its subjects to place one or more of the given figures within a familiar setting (a bedroom, a street, a bridge, etc.) and then, with certain leads, to elaborate a story from the created scene. This is a projective test, not unlike the Thematic Apperception Test (see page 71). The story provides the psychologist with imagined projections for analysis of personality and pathological disorders. The sixty-seven figures certainly furnish plenty of suggestive material: merely looking at them, the inventive mind boggles.

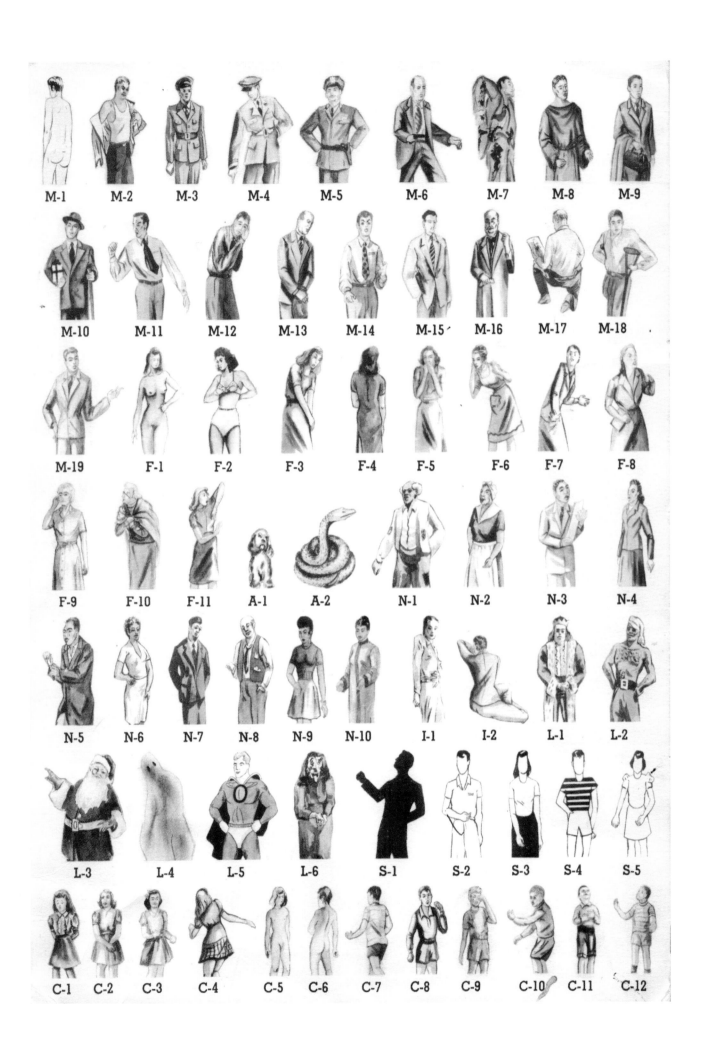

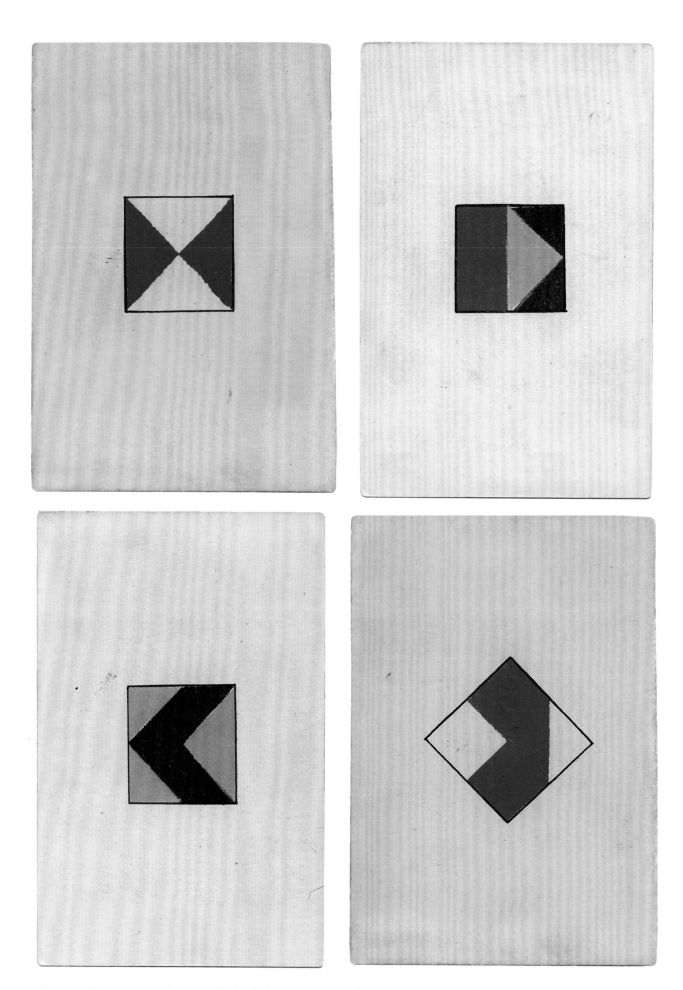

These beautiful hand-made cards were used in visualisation tests with the smaller cubes pictured on page 22.

PICTORIAL COMPLETION TEST

Seeming to combine both of his specialisms, this test was devised in the 1920s by the Chicago child psychiatrist and criminologist William Healy: its purpose was to detect incipient juvenile delinquency and 'defective or aberrational' tendencies in children. Margaret Lowenfeld (see page 24) used it for a more benign purpose: to diagnose the problems of traumatised children. Each scene has items missing; the child was asked to replace them from a number of given options. Not so much 'spot the ball' as 'supply the ball'.

C. H. STOELTING COMPANY
424 NORTH HOMAN AVENUE • CHICAGO 24, ILL., U. S. A.

America's Institution for Psychological and
Physiological Apparatus and Supplies

MANUFACTURERS OF:	TESTS FOR:
Psychological and	Psychiatrists
Physiological	Neurologists
Apparatus and Supplies	Psychologists
Precision Timers	Radiometers
Personal Aptitude Tests	Vacuum Gages
Performance Ability Tests	Kymographs
Intelligence Tests	Dynamometers
Lie Detectors	Stop Watches

This interesting firm was established in 1886. Comparatively few people realize the important role that the science of psychology has played in human affairs. Already the demand for its application to every phase of human activity of importance is now recognized by the leading Universities, Colleges, Schools and Personnel Departments.

We invite inquiries for special made-to-order apparatus as well as standard equipment.

Consultation service is entirely free and gladly given to anyone desiring to take advantage of it.

bfs/003/01

MANUAL
for

Pictorial Completion Test II
Cat. No. 46253

by

William Healy

Property of _____

_____

_____

C. H. STOELTING CO.
424 NORTH HOMAN AVENUE
CHICAGO 24, ILL., U. S. A.

Printed in U. S. A.

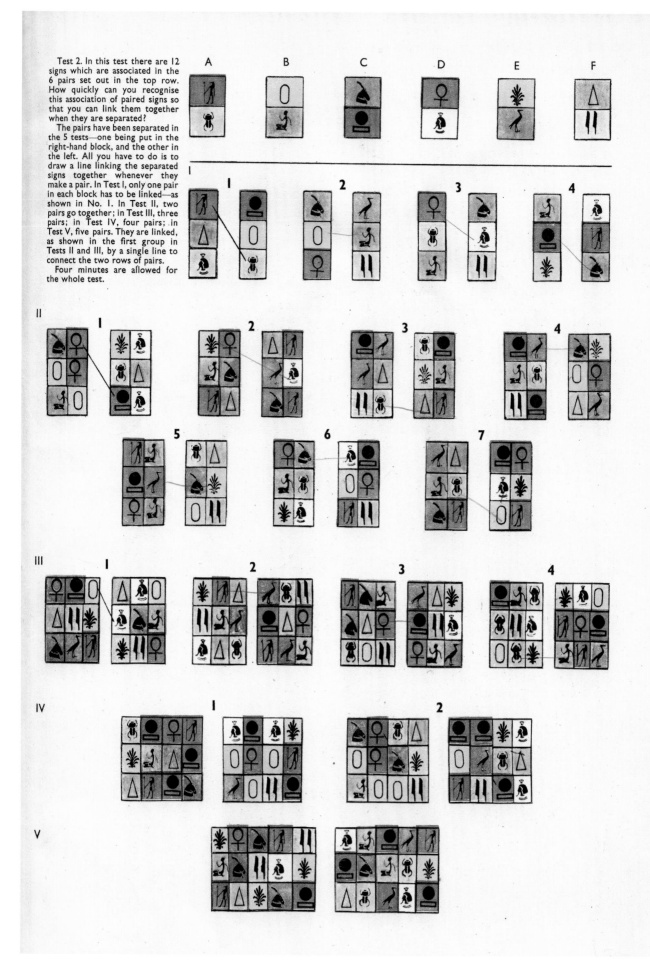

Test 2. In this test there are 12 signs which are associated in the 6 pairs set out in the top row. How quickly can you recognise this association of paired signs so that you can link them together when they are separated?

The pairs have been separated in the 5 tests—one being put in the right-hand block, and the other in the left. All you have to do is to draw a line linking the separated signs together whenever they make a pair. In Test I, only one pair in each block has to be linked—as shown in No. I. In Test II, two pairs go together; in Test III, three pairs; in Test IV, four pairs; in Test V, five pairs. They are linked, as shown in the first group in Tests II and III, by a single line to connect the two rows of pairs.

Four minutes are allowed for the whole test.

A symbol association test for assessment of recognition and connection skills.

42

Travelling case for Raven's Matrices test cards.

INTELLIGENCE AND
PERCEPTUAL SPEED TESTS

In this well-known non-verbal intelligence test, Raven's Matrices
(originally developed by John C. Raven in 1936), the initial problem is
quite easy, being based on simple visual matching: 'find the missing
section'. But tests become progressively more difficult, requiring
the subject to draw inferences about what must be the logical (or
geometric) completion of a series of diagrams. Because they do
not use words or culture-specific images (as in many projective and
questionnaire tests), tests of this diagrammatic type are considered
to be 'culture fair', i.e. they avoid cultural bias. Whether they do or
not is a moot point.

A 4

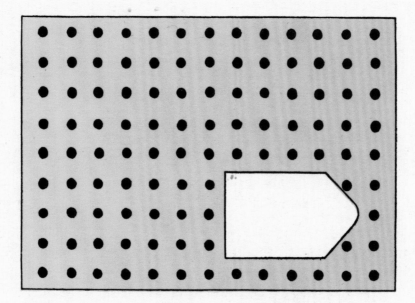

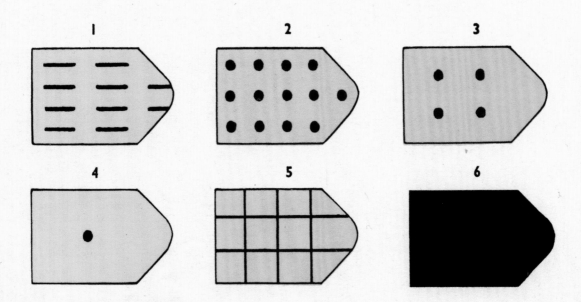

44

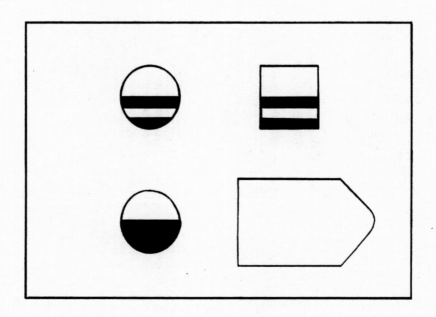

1   2   3

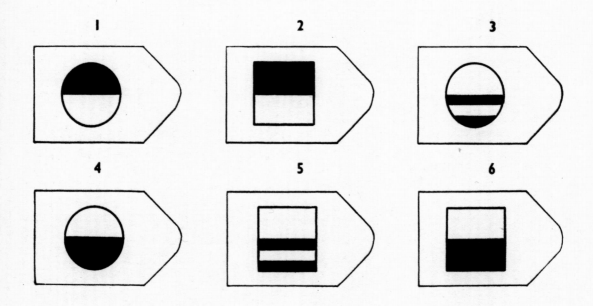

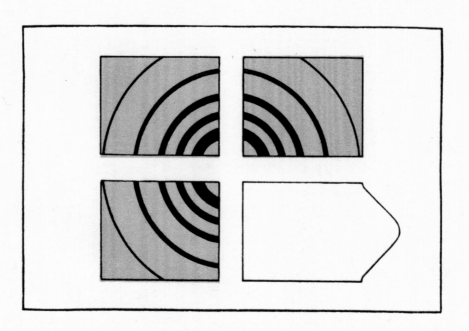

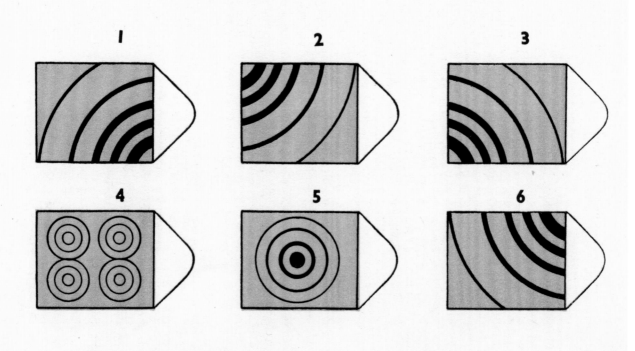

A_B 9

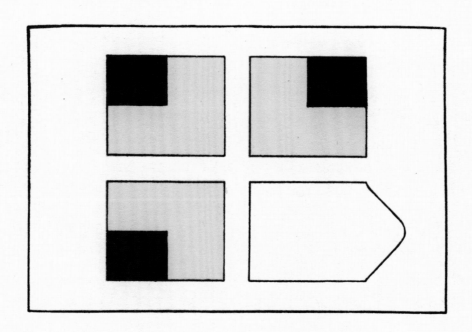

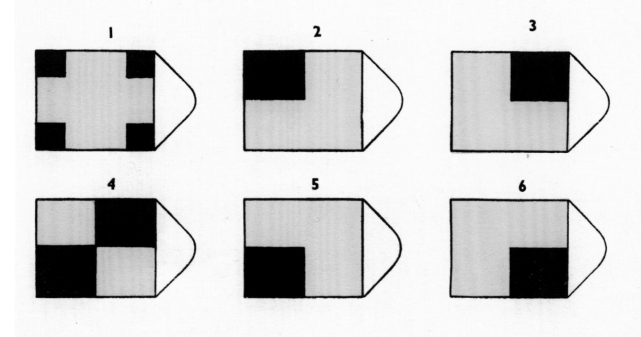

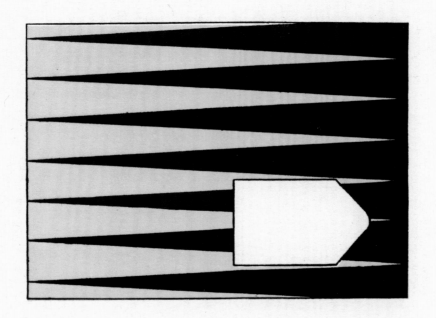

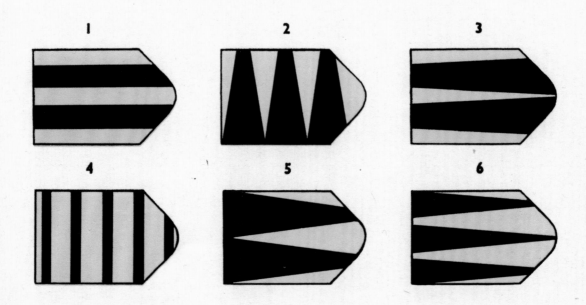

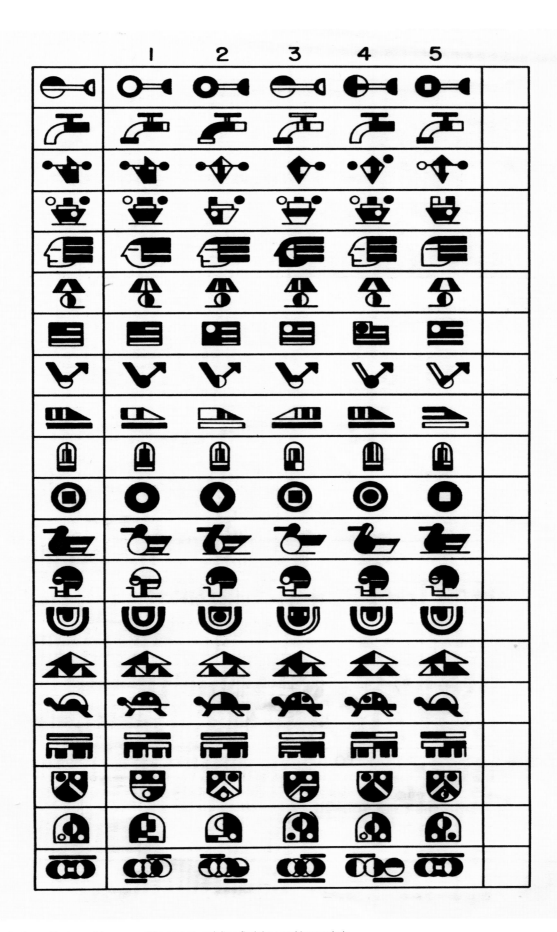

	1	2	3	4	5	

Perceptual speed tests, on this page and the next. In each line, find the matching symbols.

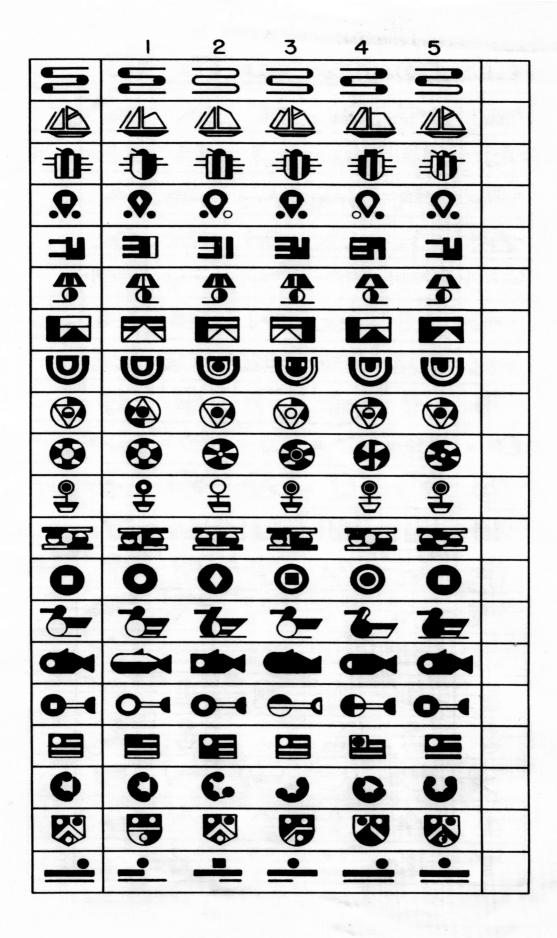

2

INKBLOTS

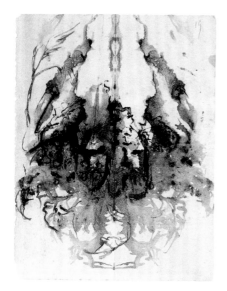

Inkblot by Victor Hugo, date unknown.

Victor Hugo, photographed by Etienne Carjat, 1876.

INKBLOTS

From Leonardo to the Surrealists, artists have been aware that arbitrary stains, blots and marks can provide the basis of imaginative pictorial experiments. The great novelist Victor Hugo, a remarkably original draughtsman, was fascinated by inkblots, and valued them as mysterious signs. It took the brilliant young Swiss psychologist Hermann Rorschach (possibly inspired by Justinus Kerner's fantastical drawings) to realise that a set of systemised symmetrical inkblots might form the basis of a revelatory projective test. His book, *Psychodiagnostik*, elaborating the idea, was published in 1921. Rorschach died the following year at 37 years of age.

Page from Justinus Kerner's *Klecksographen*, 1890.

THE GHOSTS
OF MY FRIENDS

First published in London in 1905, *The Ghosts of My Friends* was a popular variation on the autograph album, in which friends were invited to write their signature 'with a full pen of ink' along the fold of the page, then close the book to create a symmetrical blot. The results are poetic, comic and sometimes slightly sinister.

Date 2/10/10.

Name Bertha van Duren

Date January 8th 1906.

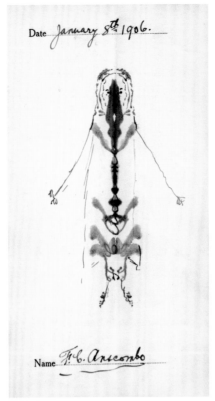

Name F. C. Anscombo

Date 28/8/10.

Name R. Berlin

Date 29th Dec. /05

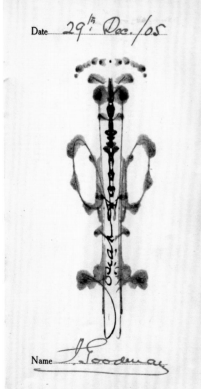

Name J. Goodman

Date Dec 29th 1905

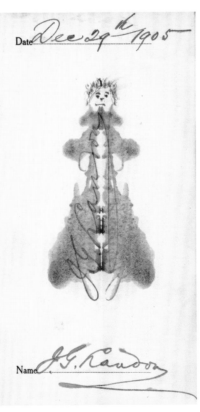

Name J. G. Kandon

Date January 28th 1906

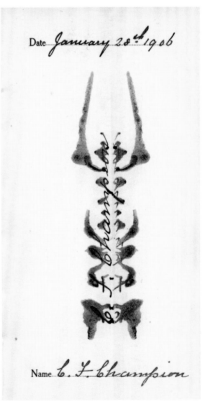

Name C. F. Champion

THE RORSCHACH INKBLOT TEST

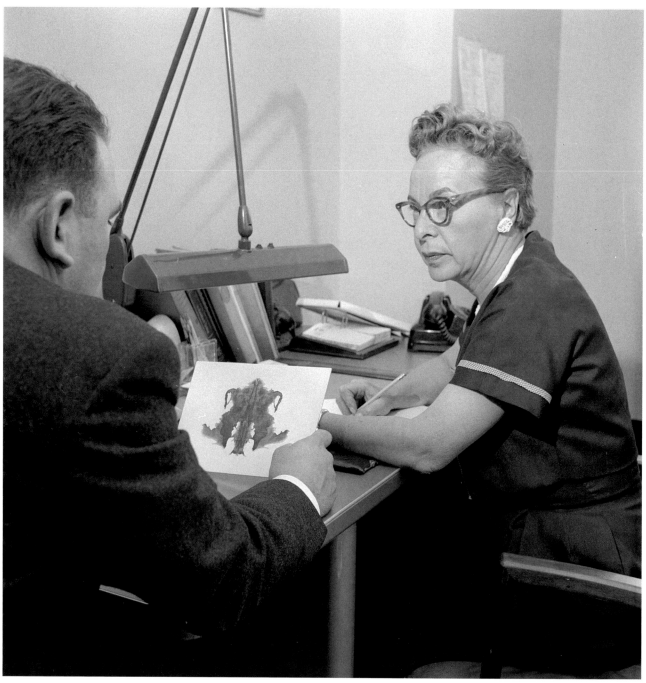

A patient taking the Rorschach inkblot test, USA, c.1951.

Hermann Rorschach in 1910. Photographer unknown.

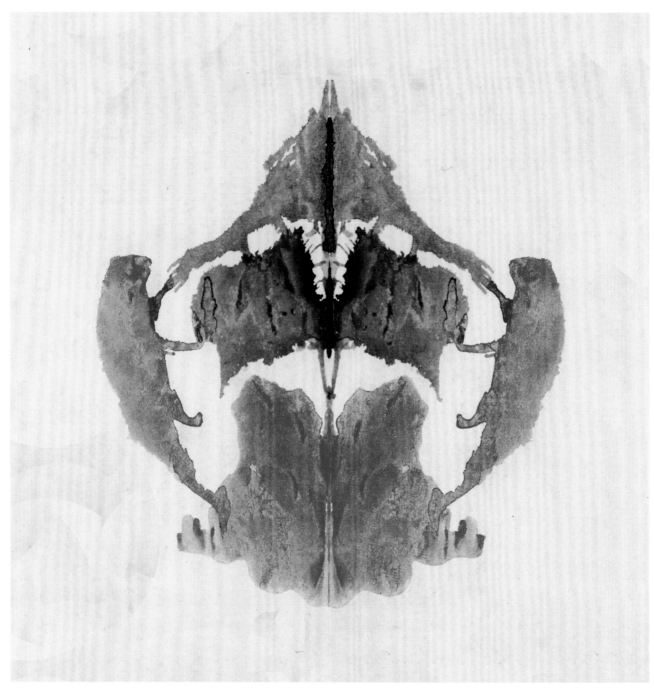

Above and on pages 59 to 62: original Rorschach inkblots.

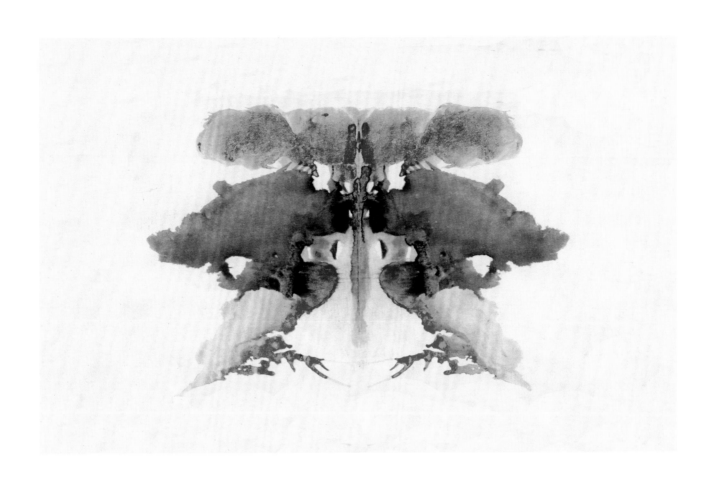

WHAT DO YOU SEE? WHAT DOES IT MEAN?

Study the inkblots on pages 66 – 70, then refer to
pages 182 - 184 for commentary and feedback.

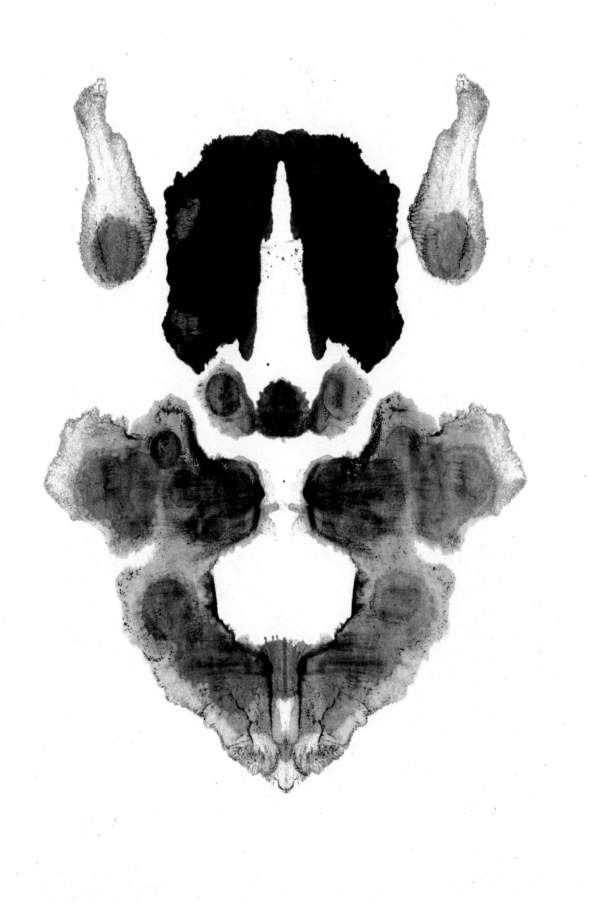

Turn to page 182.

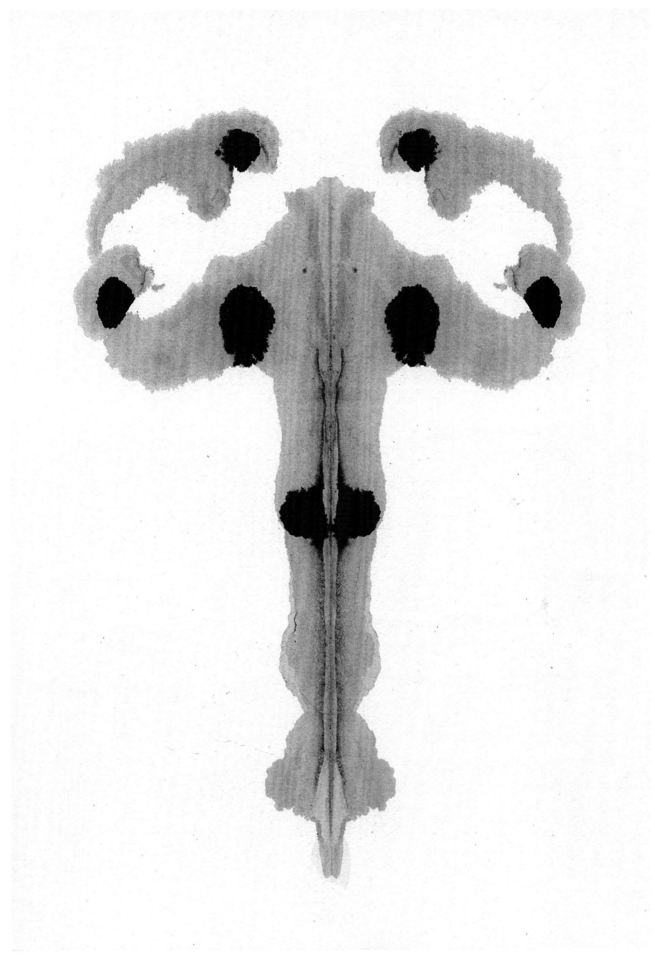

Turn to page 182.

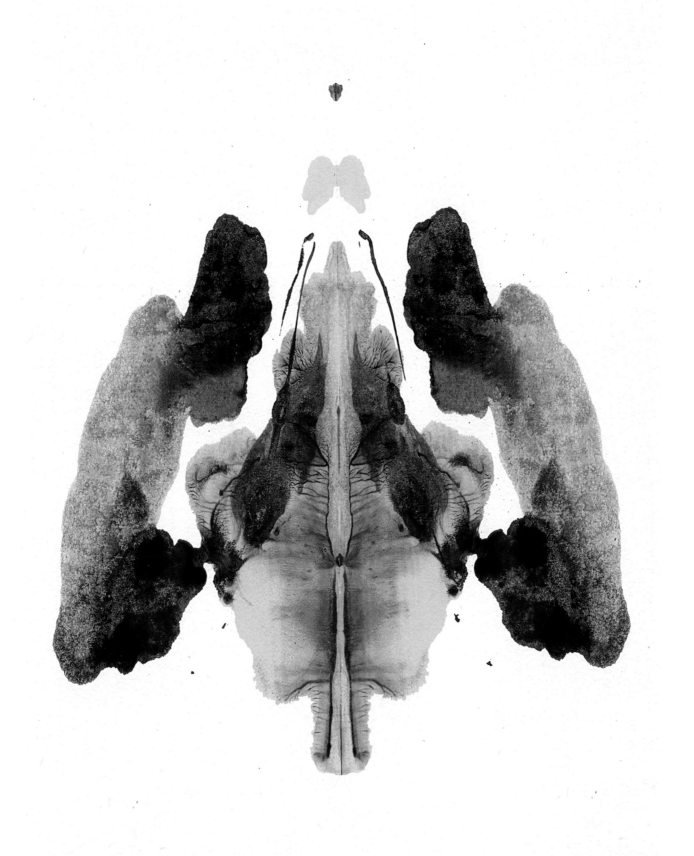

Turn to page 183.

Turn to page 183.

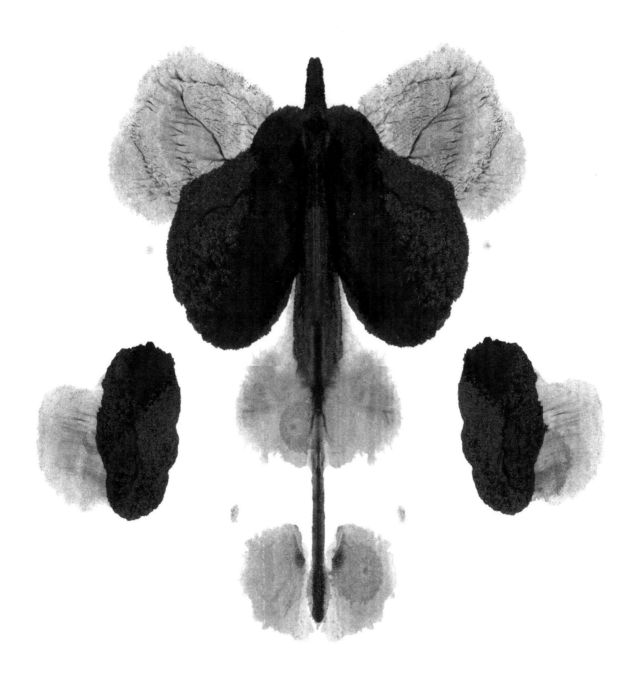

Turn to page 184.

3

THE THEMATIC APPERCEPTION TEST (TAT)

A psychologist and his patient, USA, c.1950.

THE THEMATIC APPERCEPTION TEST (TAT)

'It is not so much I read a book as that the book reads me.'
W. H. Auden

Psychiatrists and therapists have long used patients' or clients'
responses to images or pictures as the starting point for the
discovery and analysis of their inner thoughts, hidden feelings,
private fantasies and unacknowledged hopes and fears. The
Thematic Apperception Test (TAT) is a 'projective' test of this kind.
In this context 'projection' is defined as perceiving in an external
object (a picture, a story), or a figure or character, aspects of
an internal emotional or psychological condition that are often
hidden in ordinary discourse. Images used in the TAT are always
ambiguous and fraught with implication, and therefore open
to imaginative interpretation.

The examples from the original 1930s TAT (which were cut out
of contemporary magazines), shown here on pages 75 - 77, are
followed by a series of images by photographer Sarah Ainslie that
were specially commissioned for this book. What do you think is
happening with the situations shown in these pictures?

4

TEST YOUR PERSONALITY: CHECK YOUR MOOD

THE COEXISTENCE SCALES

DEVISED BY WILL HOBSON

People have their own ideas of how day-to-day life works, patterns of existence with which they are comfortable. For those who live alone, these flourish in isolation. They may be tested against rules of thumb such as, 'Everything in moderation, including moderation,' evolving slowly under the effects of reflection. But they enter a new phase when people start to cohabit and compare at first hand the way they do things. Negotiation, compromise and revelation enter the picture.

One way to depict this process is to imagine a type of behaviour as a spectrum or scale, with extreme variants at each end. People can take turns saying where they think they are on the scale and then, by answering questions about concrete examples of behaviour on this spectrum, demonstrate what this means.

Five scales follow: for Sociability, Flexibility, Empathy, Communication and Ego. In some cases, there's a question as to whether there should be more than one scale since so many things are involved, but ideally this will further stimulate conversation.

SOCIABILITY

'Friend of men, and enemy of almost every man he had to do with.'

Thomas Carlyle on the Marquis de Mirabeau, who wrote the treatise *L'Ami des hommes* (1759).

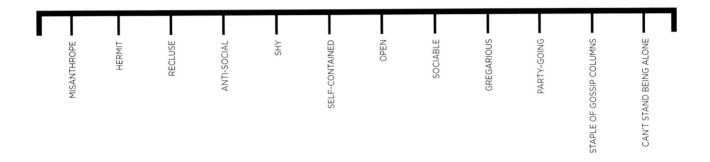

MISANTHROPE HERMIT RECLUSE ANTI-SOCIAL SHY SELF-CONTAINED OPEN SOCIABLE GREGARIOUS PARTY-GOING STAPLE OF GOSSIP COLUMNS CAN'T STAND BEING ALONE

1. If you read the morning paper, do you think of it as a solitary activity or an occasion for conversation and observations about the world?

2. Have you ever, like Beau Brummel, accepted an invitation on condition that your host promises not to tell anyone you have done so?

3. What is your view of Sir Alex Ferguson's comment, 'Kenny Dalglish has associates, but only a few friends. There's nothing wrong with that because, at the end of the day, you only need six people to carry your coffin'?

4. Do you often need to lie down after visiting/being visited?

5. If someone can't say something nice, would you, like Roseanne Barr, probably like them?

6. What's the largest number of times you've changed your outfit in a night?

7. Do you hide when the doorbell rings? Or the telephone?

8. Do you prepare notes of things to talk about?

9. Have you ever stayed too long at the fair?

10. Do you believe that laughing for no reason, as the Russian proverb has it, makes you a fool?

FLEXIBILITY

'One is merely a cork. You must let yourself go along in life like a cork in the current of the stream'. Auguste Renoir

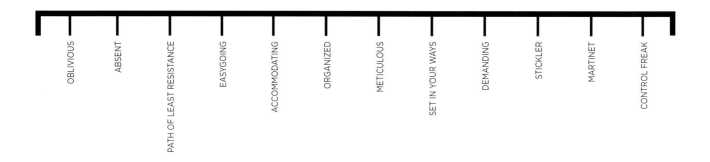

OBLIVIOUS · ABSENT · PATH OF LEAST RESISTANCE · EASYGOING · ACCOMMODATING · ORGANIZED · METICULOUS · SET IN YOUR WAYS · DEMANDING · STICKLER · MARTINET · CONTROL FREAK

1. When you go to bed, do you expect everyone else to follow suit?

2. Do you ever turn off the lights in a room without checking if someone is in there first?

3. Have you ever redecorated someone's home without them asking?

4. How many times a day do you say 'I'm so busy'?

5. Do you tend to do the easiest, most pragmatic thing – keep your mobile phone in your bra/sock, for instance – or do you like things to be just so?

6. Do you put everything on hold while you mull an idea over?

7. Do you like to go with the flow, see where it leads you?

8. Do you ever signal that you want people to leave by picking up a broom and sweeping energetically, or by taking off your shoes and starting to undress for bed?

9. Do you get anxious if your routine changes?

10. Do you constantly make remarks about people's clothes or lives, either out of concern, or otherwise?

EMPATHY

Bill Sampson (Gary Merrill): Have you no human consideration? Margo Channing (Bette Davis): Show me a human, and I might have!

From *All About Eve*, written and directed by Joseph L. Mankiewicz

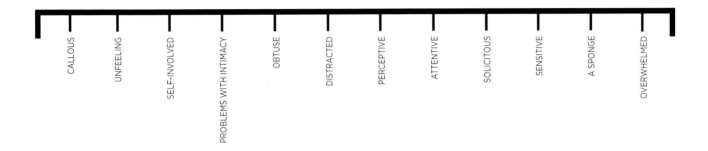

1. Are you good at giving people the chance to be nice?

2. Do you think unhappiness is contagious?

3. Do you see good manners, as Jonathan Swift said, as the art of putting people at their ease?

4. Given their reliability, are you ever tempted to prefer objects to people?

5. When someone is sharing something painful with you, do you a) avoid eye contact b) interrupt c) change the subject d) tell them it's not the end of the world e) compare their experiences with yours f) look at the TV/your phone g) immediately give practical advice h) try not to do any of the above?

6. How entitled do you feel? Do you, for instance, always assume everyone will be able to afford to eat at a restaurant of your choosing?

7. Is there someone you secretly dread to whom you are similar?

8. Do you think shyness is an essential part of growing up, a sort of protective fluid that allows personalities to develop properly?

9. Emil White entitled one of his paintings: '*Strangers of the world unite, you have nothing to lose but your own loneliness!*' Could that ever be what you feel?

10. To change perspective entirely, would you be more inclined to go into the desert or to surround yourself with animals?

COMMUNICATION

'It's impossible not to communicate. You cannot be for or against it. You can only do it more or less well – by your own standards or by other people's – but you can't not do it.'

Adam Phillips, *Monogamy*, 1996

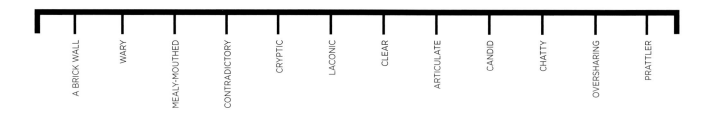

A BRICK WALL | WARY | MEALY-MOUTHED | CONTRADICTORY | CRYPTIC | LACONIC | CLEAR | ARTICULATE | CANDID | CHATTY | OVERSHARING | PRATTLER

1. Do you have a safe word? If so, is it as sublime as that of John Cena's character in the film *Sisters*, whose safe word is 'Keep going'?

2. Would great nastiness make your life easier? Specifically, do you find yourself saying 'yes' to other people because, as the artist Thomas Schütte has said, 'You don't have to explain a yes'?

3. Do you think the ideal time to announce your big news – engagement, pregnancy, etc. – is someone else's big day?

4. What are the mixed messages you most like to give?

5. If you had slept with ten thousand people, would you, like Georges Simenon, put this down to a need to communicate?

6. Do you feel emotions welling up in you but think that expressing them would 'rock the boat'?

7. Do you talk to your reflection in the mirror
a) ever b) occasionally c) so habitually it could have a sign saying 'We Meet Again'?

8. Do you feel human-robot interactions – at supermarket self-service checkouts, for instance – should be
a) more human-friendly b) more robot-friendly c) avoided?

9. How many unsent emails are there in your drafts folder?

10. Groucho Marx said of S. J. Perelman's *Dawn Ginsbergh's Revenge*, 'From the moment I picked up your book until I laid it down, I was convulsed with laughter. Someday I intend reading it.' Do you have a similar way with pleasantries?

EGO

'At the age of six I wanted to be a cook. At seven I wanted to be Napoleon. And my ambition has been growing steadily ever since.'

Salvador Dalí

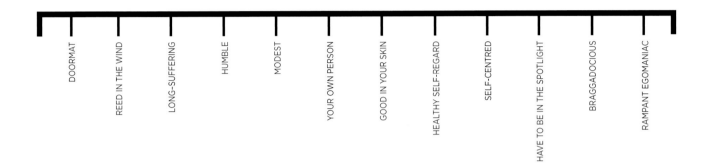

DOORMAT | REED IN THE WIND | LONG-SUFFERING | HUMBLE | MODEST | YOUR OWN PERSON | GOOD IN YOUR SKIN | HEALTHY SELF-REGARD | SELF-CENTRED | HAVE TO BE IN THE SPOTLIGHT | BRAGGADOCIOUS | RAMPANT EGOMANIAC

1. Would you, like Herbert Lom, be tempted to choose as one of your records for Desert Island Discs an eight-minute standing ovation for yourself? Or, like Otto Preminger, your autobiography as your book?

2. Given how averse most people are to confrontation, do you think it makes sense to be as temperamental as possible?

3. When you have people round, would you consider entertaining them by reading out extracts from your long and ever-changing will?

4. Do you, like Napoleon in Woody Allen's *Love and Death*, have a 'great walk'?

5. Have you ever responded, 'Fine', when someone's asked you to do something, when 'fine' is the last thing it could ever be?

6. Have you ever sat on a piano to make your legs look long?

7. Have you ever banned someone from being in a photograph with you because they're not attractive enough?

8. Do you take a selfie of yourself every night to preserve the moment?

9. After your death is there a chance you might become a god?

10. Like Ronnie Scott, are you never wrong except on the very rare occasions when you've thought you were wrong but you weren't?

	Mother's	Father's	Neither's
Nose			
Eyes			
Ears			
Smile			
Laugh			
Voice			
Fillings			
Smell			
Expressions			
Allergies			
Body Language			
Sense Of Humour			
Temper			
Jokes			
Sayings			
Criminal Record			
Dance Moves			
Taste			
Football Team			
Qualms			
Driving			
Fashion Sense			
Pet Hates			
Skills			
Neuroses			
Vices			
Phobias			
Good Habits			
Bad Habits			
Qualifications			
Idiosyncrasies			
Philosophy			
Religion			
Morals			
Politics			

Personality Inventory: What Comes from Whom? This page and the one opposite were devised for the *Identity* exhibition at the Wellcome Trust in 2009.

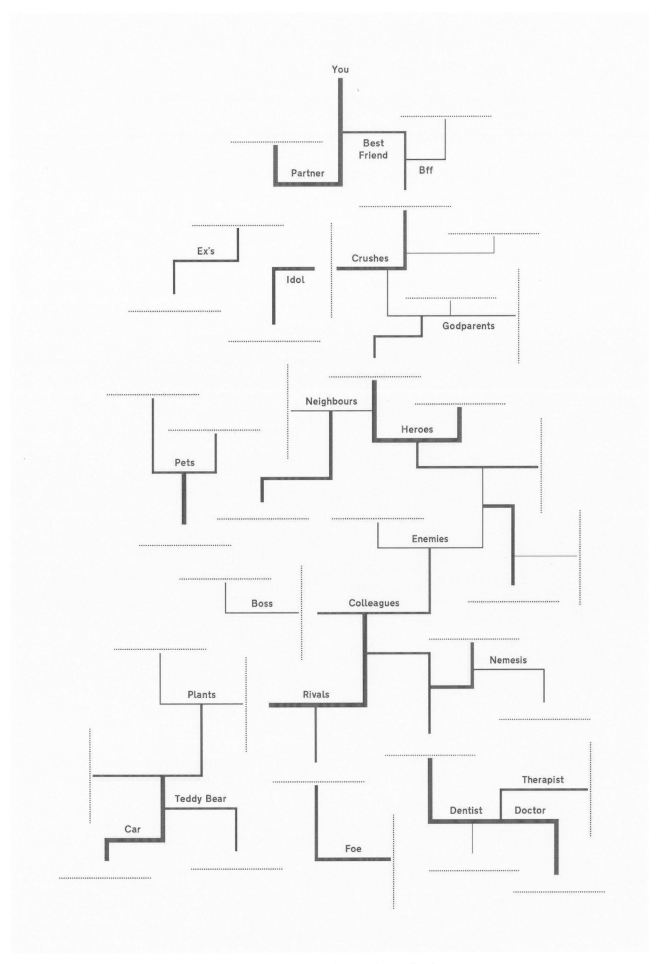

Personality Tree: Starting from the bottom, fill in the names relevant to you until you reach yourself at the top.

THE STORY TEST

This is a type of test that has been popular with many diagnosticians, for purposes similar to those behind the Thematic Apperception Test (TAT). The test entails inventing a story with alternative possibilities of development. The story here, adapted from a real test, has much in common with John Bunyan's *The Pilgrim's Progress*, which, interestingly, came to him in a dream.

This is the most simple type of story test, at each point offering only a limited number of ways to progress. Turn to page 184 for interpretations.

1. Imagine that you are entering a forest

Is it light or dark?

Do you see a path?

2. Begin walking through the forest

You see a cup. What does it look like?

What do you do with it?

3. You continue through the forest and come across water

What does the water look like?

Is it moving?

How deep is it?

You need to cross the water. How do you do this?

4. You then encounter a bear.

What sort of bear is it?

What is it doing?

You need to carry on. How do you get around the bear?

5. You reach a clearing. You can see a beach.

Can you see any people?

If so, how far away are they?

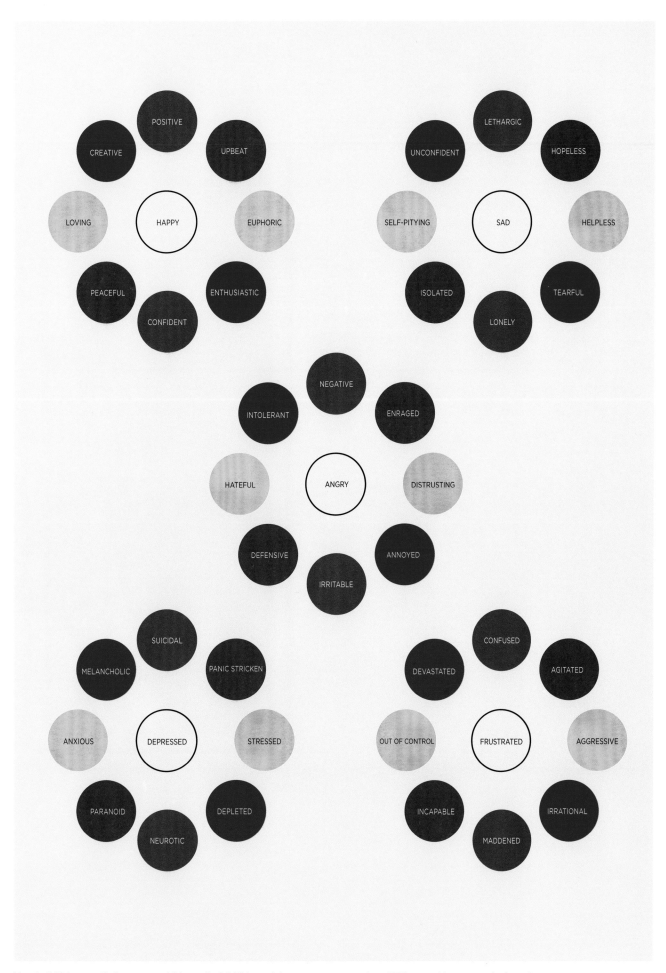

Moods: Which constellation are you visiting today? Whichever it is, are you on every planet? Things could get worse (or better).

THE FEELING TEST

Psychotherapists and counsellors often present their clients with an image asking them to identify, at the moment of asking, with one or other of the figures whose various attitudes may seem to represent prevailing moods or dispositions. This test may provide some indication of your present condition of self-awareness or self-esteem; and even if treated with a degree of wry and self-reflexive irony it may stimulate thoughtful reflection and commentary useful to the therapy.

This test is still widely used.

The drawing on the facing page, by an unknown psychologist, is a version popular among therapists.

All other versions are by the artist Adam Dant.

The Shopping Mall. Which figure do you identify with? Turn to page 185.

The House of Personalities. Which figure are you? Turn to page 185.

The Climbing Frame. Which figure are you? Turn to page 185.

MODERN LIFE
FRUSTRATIONS TEST

We live in a world that constantly finds ways to frustrate us. Television, magazines, films and advertising (especially advertising) present us with an interminably perfect image of things impossible to achieve: we'll never be as beautiful, as rich, as perfectly dressed or as happy as those who inhabit the looking-glass world of screen and glossy page. We know that, of course, and though it doesn't stop us dreaming, we live, more or less happily, with the realities of our everyday existence. But the everyday of modern life provides us with a multitude of ordinary frustrations, to which we may respond in a variety of ways – with varying degrees of aggression, for example, or with other quite different defence mechanisms, such as a tendency often to take the blame for the situation on ourselves, or to deny that we have been inconvenienced or frustrated at all.

Adam Dant's comic sequence, which follows, is inspired by a famous projective test developed by the psychologist Saul Rosenzweig, the purpose of which is to gauge the extent of a subject's aggression in response to commonplace frustrations. The test consists of a number of cartoon images featuring two figures: one responsible for a situation that induces frustration or annoyance in the other, and whose utterance intensifies it, and the other whose empty speech bubble invites the subject to provide a verbal response. Degrees of latent aggression would be judged in accordance with the type of responses exhibited (whether recurrently aggressive or non-aggressive, or apologetic, or denying frustration) and the direction of aggression (outward towards the 'frustator' or inward towards the self). These ways of reacting may well link to the bias towards extraversion or introversion in the subject's personality.

Adopting the format of the test, Dant's sequence picks up humorously on the many and various annoying events which conspire to create irritation and frustration as commonplace aspects of any average 'day in the life'. You may find yourself tending, characteristically, to respond in one way or another; or find that your responses vary according to the nature of the scenario, or your mood. It has to be said that some of these situations might try the patience of a saint, and justifiably bring out the devil in you, and that in others, sweet reason may inspire saintly forbearance.

Three images from the twenty-four in the *Rosenzweig Picture-Frustration Study* (1978). The variations on this theme on pages 108 – 111 were created by Adam Dant.

WILSON-PATTERSON ATTITUDE INVENTORY

Name.. Sex ....

Occupation.. Age ....

Date...................................

Clubs and affiliations...

WHICH OF THE FOLLOWING DO YOU FAVOUR OR BELIEVE IN?

(Circle 'Yes' or 'No'. If absolutely uncertain, circle '?'. There are no right or wrong answers; do not discuss; just give your first reaction. Answer all items).

1 death penalty	Yes	?	No	26 birth control	Yes	?	No
2 evolution theory	Yes	?	No	27 coloured immigration	Yes	?	No
3 white superiority	Yes	?	No	28 self-denial	Yes	?	No
4 working mothers	Yes	?	No	29 cousin marriage	Yes	?	No
5 Divine law	Yes	?	No	30 Bible truth	Yes	?	No
6 pornography	Yes	?	No	31 jazz	Yes	?	No
7 disarmament	Yes	?	No	32 military drill	Yes	?	No
8 learning Latin	Yes	?	No	33 inborn conscience	Yes	?	No
9 smoking pot	Yes	?	No	34 co-education	Yes	?	No
10 royalty	Yes	?	No	35 Sabbath observance	Yes	?	No
11 legal abortion	Yes	?	No	36 computer music	Yes	?	No
12 Church authority	Yes	?	No	37 casual living	Yes	?	No
13 conventional clothes	Yes	?	No	38 women judges	Yes	?	No
14 fluoridation	Yes	?	No	39 patriotism	Yes	?	No
15 modern art	Yes	?	No	40 easy divorce	Yes	?	No
16 strict rules	Yes	?	No	41 school uniforms	Yes	?	No
17 corporal punishment	Yes	?	No	42 student pranks	Yes	?	No
18 miracles	Yes	?	No	43 licensing laws	Yes	?	No
19 socialism	Yes	?	No	44 teenage drivers	Yes	?	No
20 hippies	Yes	?	No	45 chastity	Yes	?	No
21 chaperones	Yes	?	No	46 striptease shows	Yes	?	No
22 straitjackets	Yes	?	No	47 white lies	Yes	?	No
23 racial segregation	Yes	?	No	48 empire building	Yes	?	No
24 moral training	Yes	?	No	49 mixed marriage	Yes	?	No
25 censorship	Yes	?	No	50 suicide	Yes	?	No

Published by NFER Publishing Company Ltd. All rights reserved.
© NFER 1975. Printed in Great Britain.

The Wilson-Patterson Attitude Inventory (WPAI), 1975, designed to measure people's attitude to conservatism.

5

WRITERS IMAGINE QUESTIONNAIRES

A psychoanalyst listens to a patient digging into her past at the New York Psychoanalytic Institute Treatment Centre in New York, 1956.

WRITERS IMAGINE QUESTIONNAIRES

The American Declaration of Independence famously states that it is a truth self-evident that 'the pursuit of happiness' is 'an inalienable right'. But how do you measure personal fulfilment? All over the world there are thousands upon thousands who, seeking that elusive state of perfect contentment, go to shrinks, therapists and counsellors of all persuasions, employ personal trainers, sit at the feet of mystical gurus, turn to religion, or listen, rapt, to meditation teachers on CDs and DVDs. Getting people to feel fulfilled is a highly profitable business.

Contentment is such a valuable commodity that we feel we ought to be able to measure it. There are so many variables – heredity and temperament, circumstances, the will to be happy, and so on – that no method has been able to do more than arrive at a vague approximation. In fact, most people most of the time, it seems, think themselves reasonably happy. Research indicates that if you ask people, anywhere in the world, and of all types and condition, to rate their happiness out of ten, the answer will be seven. For this part of the book, we have asked writers who are not psychologists to invent tests and questionnaires that might provide some new ideas about everyone's search for that elusive condition: contentment.

THE CB IDENTITY QUESTIONNAIRE (CBIQ)

BY CHARLES BOYLE

Your response to the questions should take the form of a), b) or c).

a) You identify with this statement, absolutely.
b) This statement does apply to you, but only in part or sometimes.
c) You don't recognise yourself in this statement.

If I had a different name, I would be a different person.

I like dressing up in clothes I wouldn't normally wear.

I remember almost nothing of my childhood.

I think certain people are taller than me, even though in fact they're not.

When I'm in company with other people, I find myself copying their mannerisms or habits of speech.

I often imagine being someone of the opposite gender.

I enjoy throwing things away.

Sometimes I feel I've been hacked into by someone else.

I see myself as a river, not a tree.

In most arguments, I can see right on both sides.

I often change my mind.

I'm happy to take psychotropic drugs.

When I hear someone in the street shouting 'Stop thief!', I think it's me they're after.

Tracing adult behaviour to childhood trauma is missing the point.

In films and books, I'm hopeless at following plots; I get distracted by the scenery.

I deal with fear and pain by imagining that I'm someone who feels no fear or pain.

When I answer psychological questionnaires, I tick the boxes that don't apply to me.

Mostly a, b, or c ? To discover what your results signify, turn to page 185.

SIX TYPES OF READING FOR A BETTER KIND OF LIFE

BY ROBERT McCRUM

ROMANCE: Lunatics, Lovers and Poets

Which book or poem would you most like to read in bed?

Name the English word you find most sensuous.

What's your favourite novel?

Which book might you use for a seduction – *Love in a Cold Climate* by Nancy Mitford or *Lolita* by Vladimir Nabokov?

Would you rather have a date with Oscar Wilde (*The Ballad of Reading Gaol*) or Anita Loos (*Gentlemen Prefer Blondes*)?

WORK: A Hard Day's Night

Would you prefer to read:

Christopher Marlowe or William Shakespeare?

Emily Dickinson or Virginia Woolf?

P. G. Wodehouse or Henry James?

Walt Whitman or T. S. Eliot?

Ian Fleming or John Le Carré?

IDENTITY: Who Goes There?

Would you prefer to be 'Anonymous' or to use a pseudonym?

In Shakespeare's *Hamlet*, do you identify with Laertes or Horatio?

Would you rather meet William Thackeray's Becky Sharp or Emily Brontë's Cathy Heathcliff?

Which writers make you cry?

Do you prefer your writing paper to be lined or plain?

Which member of the crew of the Pequod in *Moby Dick* would you be?

Would you rather be a minor character in Oscar Wilde's *The Picture of Dorian Gray* or in Thomas Hardy's *Jude the Obscure*?

SOLITUDE: No Man Is an Island

Would you prefer:

to read a stage play or a novel?

the seaside or the country?

to perform as Bottom or Coriolanus?

to play Prospero or Lear?

to be Mr. Darcy or Robinson Crusoe?

to parody a page of *Dracula* or one from *On the Road*?

When you re-read *Catcher in the Rye*, do you

regret your teenage years?

turn to a long work of horticultural history?

think that J. D. Salinger is a weirdo?

book a flight to Manhattan?

ABROAD: A Peak in Darien

What's your favourite travel book?

Whose house, abroad, would you most like to visit?

Would you prefer to stay with Somerset Maugham in Villa Mauresque or with Winston Churchill at Chequers?

Choose between *A Passage to India* by E.M. Forster and *Kim* by Rudyard Kipling.

Choose between *Heart of Darkness* by Joseph Conrad and *A Bend in the River* by V. S. Naipaul.

Would you rather have a drink with Ernest Hemingway in Key West or an evening with Jack Kerouac in Greenwich Village?

Choose between *Roughing It* by Mark Twain and *The Amateur Emigrant* by Robert Louis Stevenson.

ILL HEALTH: For Whom the Bell Tolls

Would you prefer to be treated by Somerset Maugham or Conan Doyle?

Would you prefer to have been D. H. Lawrence or John Keats?

When you're under the weather, do you take comfort in a favourite novel or thrillers?

Choose between *Frankenstein* by Mary Shelley and *Slaughterhouse Five* by Kurt Vonnegut.

Would you choose to be visited in hospital by Hilary Mantel or Margaret Atwood?

Would you want your last conversation to be with Clive James or Christopher Hitchens?

Would you like to be read to by Stephen King or Anne Tyler?

Dr Alfred Kinsey interviewing a mother, USA, c.1955.

EVERYDAY GUILT TEST (EGT)

BY KATE PULLINGER

This test, to be done in the morning, will help you and/or your subject determine the impact that guilt has on everyday life.

When you get up in the morning do you

a) wish you had got up earlier?
b) wish you had slept better?
c) wish you didn't have to get up at all?
d) simply get up and get on with the day?

While you eat your breakfast do you

a) feel bad about the fact that all you eat in the morning is sugar?
b) shout at the radio then worry about who has heard you?
c) plan the rest of the day's meals carefully in order to achieve a balanced diet, then remember those plans later after you've eaten?
d) complete yesterday's newspaper crossword while humming your favourite tune?

When you pick up your phone and discover eight new messages from your least favourite parent/work colleague/classmate do you

a) delete the messages without reading them?
b) wish that person had never been born then regret that wish?
c) tell yourself you'll deal with this problem later?
d) answer all the messages while remaining calm?

When you get in your car in order to drive to work/school/the bar do you

a) look at your bicycle and wonder why you thought buying it would mean you would ride it?
b) remember that promise you made last night to give your neighbour a lift but drive off without them anyway?
c) think about how car emissions are destroying the world and how you are powerless to do anything about it?
d) pop on the radio to your favourite hits station and groove your way through town?

Score 4 for option a), 3 for b), 2 for c) and 1 for d). Then total your scores and turn to page 185 to determine your guilt level.

THE SEX QUESTIONNAIRE

BY NEIL BARTLETT

There are twenty-five questions in this questionnaire, but you don't have to answer them all – just the ones you fancy. They are all about sex.

PART ONE: QUESTIONS ABOUT YOU

1. Would you say you are generally frank about sex while you are doing it, or when you are talking about it, or both?

2. Would you like to be more frank?

3. Which would you say has had the most influence on you: your best sexual experience, or your worst sexual experience? What was that?

4. What's the biggest problem you have with sex these days? Would you say this is your problem, or a problem caused by society in general?

5. Which of the following words or phrases best describes your sex life ? (circle the ones you've chosen)
unforeseen / uneventful / unnatural / unlovely / unconventional / unimaginative / unpaid / unbearable unpredictable / unprincipled / unlikely / utterly wonderful / I don't have a sex life.

6. Alfred C. Kinsey insisted that his researchers never implied or suggested that they objected to any type of sexual behaviour. If you had worked for him, what type or types of sexual behaviour would you have had to admit that you do personally object to?

7. What are you most proud of in your sex life, these days?

8. And most ashamed of?

9. Would having better sex make you a better person?

10. Would being a feminist make you have better sex?

11. Is the whole idea of 'better' sex a red herring? What word would you use?

12. When the future looks back at you, do you think it will categorise you as a pioneer, a typical example, an exception, a symptom or a freak – or as something else entirely?

PART TWO: QUESTIONS ABOUT US

13. According to the authors of the British 1994 National Survey of Sexual Attitudes and Lifestyles, *We have not yet moved into a culture which tolerates sexual variety*. Do you think that statement is still true of the country in which you live?

14. If you think it is still true, how many years do you think it will be before things move on? Can you suggest any specific action that might help bring that about?

15. If you think your country does now tolerate sexual variety, do you think that's a good thing? Why – or why not?

16. Continuing in this vein, please write a true statement which includes at least three of the following words or phrases:
    JOY / SHARE/ REGRET / SHAME / BODY / BODIES / HOPE / TRANSGENDER / CHILDREN / THESE DAYS
    IN THE PAST / IN THE FUTURE / MORE / FEWER / TOO MANY / TOO FEW / ALL / STRUGGLE / SEX
    WOMEN / HOMOSEXUALS / MEN / PEOPLE / PLEASURE / NEVER / EVENTUALLY / IN MY LIFETIME
    EVERYONE

17. Whose job – if anyone's – do you think it should be to teach people about sex?

18. Has anyone ever taught you anything useful about sex ? If so, can you say where and when and with whom that lesson took place?

19. Who would you like to pass what you learned on to?

20. A big question, but an important one: does pornography help?

21. In 1927 Bronislaw Malinowski wrote a book called *Sex and Repression in Savage Society*. If you were going to write a book about how sex works these days – or about how it doesn't work, these days – what title would you give it?

22. If you could change one thing about your identity, and visit one other place and time in order to have sex there, where would you time-travel to, and as whom?

23. If you could change one thing about the way women have sex – or are allowed, assumed, forbidden or encouraged to have sex, these days – what would it be?

24. If you could change one thing about the way men have sex, what would it be?

25. And finally – and perhaps most importantly . . .

26. If you could ask other people just one question of your own about sex, what would that question be?

These questions first appeared in Neil Bartlett's artwork WOULD YOU MIND?, which was commissioned by the Wellcome Collection for its exhibition *The Institute of Sexology* in London in 2015. After the exhibition closed, every single one of 19,287 completed questionnaires were archived in the Wellcome Library, where they are now fully available to future researchers into the history of sex.

The late Jane Coleridge, psychoanalytic psychotherapist. Photograph from the series *Head Space: Photographs of Psychotherapeutic Environments*, by Nick Cunard, 2003.

THE 'MATTER IN THE WRONG PLACE' TEST

BY M. H. YORKE

Carl Jung believed that matter in the wrong place is dirt. 'People get dirty through too much civilization', he wrote. 'Whenever we touch nature, we get clean'.

Select a response to each of the following scenarios as honestly as you can. Do not spend too much time considering them – often the first answer that comes to mind is the best one.

It is your main holiday of the year – a holiday that you badly need – and you are shown to your hotel room. Immediately you are aware of a crowing cockerel.
a) You welcome this sound for its refreshing rusticity.
b) You sense it may pose a problem.
c) You know it will pose a problem.
d) You ask the hotel's proprietor if there's anything that can be done about it.

You win first prize in a raffle and are to spend a fortnight on a desert island attended by someone who scarcely speaks.
a) You think that fourteen days on your own with no talking is just what's required.
b) You're not entirely sure whether it's such an interesting prospect.
c) You know you will be bored within hours.
d) The thought fills you with panic and dread.

You awake out of sorts. You knock over a glass; stub your toe in a place where you haven't stubbed it before; nearly cause a road accident on your way to work.
a) You say to yourself: I'm out of sync with the 'matter' around me.
b) You have a vague sense of unease, a feeling that everything is conspiring against you.
c) You say to yourself that you must be tired and that it might be a good idea to have an early night tonight.

There is a horoscope in your magazine/periodical.

a) You practise delayed gratification, waiting until the page is reached before reading it.

b) Invariably you identify with something in the text specific to your star sign.

c) As your eye wanders over the page you can't help thinking that other texts may have some relevance.

d) You pass over it without looking.

Your partner adopts the annoying habit of turning on the kettle most times they walk past it.

a) You practise 'live and let live'.

b) You seek to practise 'live and let live'.

c) You politely explain to your partner that there is little advantage in keeping water close to boiling point in this way.

d) You seek to impose a ban, to nip this insidious habit in the bud. It could well lead to other bad habits, after all.

You don't get on with your neighbour. It's an almost impossible situation.

a) You wonder whether the neighbour might be some sort of archetype, a manifestation of the collective unconscious.

b) You canvass other neighbours to test the water, thereby establishing how he/she is perceived by others in the vicinity.

c) You begin to keep a diary, carefully documenting incidents that at a later date may help you to press a case.

When you think of your own impending demise. You see it as:

a) A great adventure.

b) A goal.

c) A release.

d) A sad finale.

Score 1 for option a), 2 for b), 3 for c) and 4 for d). Then total your score and turn to page 185.

Donna Bassin, PhD, psychotherapist, New York, 2009. Photograph by psychiatrist Sebastian Zimmermann.

A LIKELY STORY

BY WILL EAVES

The object of this exercise is not to attempt the task of defining probabilities, but to provide a way to assess the respondent's perception of priorities and possibilities in his or her life.

Here are a number of statements-in-threes. Have a go at ordering each group of three, and feel free to annotate your choices or express reservations. There is no right order. What will seem obvious or important or applicable to some may not be so to others, and it may be felt that a strong element of fanciful or magical thinking is involved in many of the statements.

The order of preference is the starting-point for a discussion.

AT HOME

If I lived with excruciating pain, I would not be able to cope.
If I become ill, I still try to eat properly.
If I can just talk to someone, I ought to be fine.

If the house is clean, I feel better.
If the house is dirty sometimes, I do not think it matters.
If I see a mouse in the kitchen, I call Pest Control.

If my neighbour has a fall, it means extra responsibility for me.
If I have to do small repairs, I worry about bigger things.
If my partner had an affair, I could get over it in time.

If I am feeling low, I avoid official correspondence.
If I'm happy, I mind less about money and bills.
If there is an unexpected knock at the door, I freeze.

AT WORK

I can learn difficult things as long as they are explained properly.
My time is valuable even if I'm not paid for it.
It is too late for me to learn how to manipulate new technology.

When people in authority smile at me, it's a rare but encouraging sign.
Salary negotiations go better if you're physically attractive.
The powerful prefer people who will always be grateful to them.

Letters after a name are evidence of something, I suppose.
It's important that I feel I'm doing a useful job.
I don't personally agree with what's happening, but I daren't complain.

I have made important friends through my work.
I make mistakes, so I'm reluctant to judge others.
I do not see the point of trade unions.

AT LARGE

A catastrophe grows more and more likely, so why recycle?
'Cultivate your garden' is a good rule-of-thumb.
I find it relaxing to think about outer space.

It pays to keep abreast of current affairs.
I vote out of habit rather than conviction.
If I get involved in local politics, I will end up on camera.

I am sorry for the poor but I think I deserve what I have.
My children are safer with me than at any other time.
It is OK to let the kids run wild once in a while.

Something will prevent the human race coming to an end.
It isn't always nice to say what I really think about the future.
Accidents can involve people who are good drivers.

THE SHYNESS QUESTIONNAIRE (TSQ)

BY CHARLES BOYLE

Choose option a) or option b) for each question. (In cases where you feel neither would be your ideal option, just go with the one that feels more appropriate.)

A ten-day vacation at: a) Las Vegas or b) a meditation retreat?

The magician needs someone from the audience to help him with his next trick. Do you a) put up your hand or b) stare down at your knees?

You a) haven't blushed since you were eleven years old or b) blush frequently?

You discover a new planet and get to name it: after a) yourself or b) the family pet?

Talking with someone you find attractive, you tell them a) they have beautiful eyes or b) you like their name?

Just one slice of cake is left on the plate. To take it, do you need a) zero or b) three invitations?

Lost in the city and needing directions, do you a) ask the first person who comes along or b) buy a map?

In meetings, are you a) among the first or b) among the last to speak?

If you were a writer, would you be a) a playwright or b) a novelist?

A shopkeeper gives you change from a £10 note, but you think you paid with a £20 note. Do you a) make a scene or b) shrug and walk away?

T-shirts: do you prefer them a) with slogans or b) plain?

Is someone looking for you at a party most likely to find you a) singing karaoke or b) reading the spines of the books on the shelves?

When making love, do you prefer the lights a) on or b) off?

The queue for security at the airport is a mile long. Do you a) cut to the front, claiming your flight leaves in ten minutes, or b) take your place at the back?

Would you apply for a job in a) the sales department or b) the IT department?

Are you more likely to answer this questionnaire a) in company with others or b) in private?

Note down how many a) and how many b) options you chose. Then turn to page 186.

Dr. Brooks (Barry Sullivan) and Liza Elliott (Ginger Rogers) in the film *Lady in the Dark* directed by Mitchell, Leisen, 1944.

Mark Epstein, MD, psychotherapist, New York, 2012. Photograph by psychiatrist Sebastian Zimmermann.

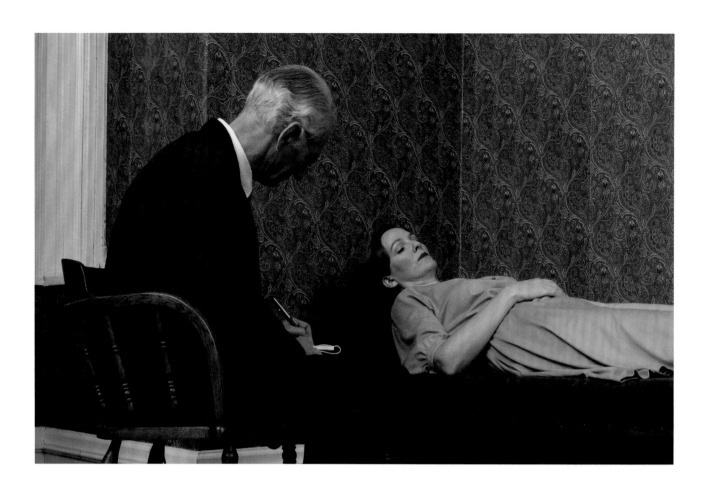

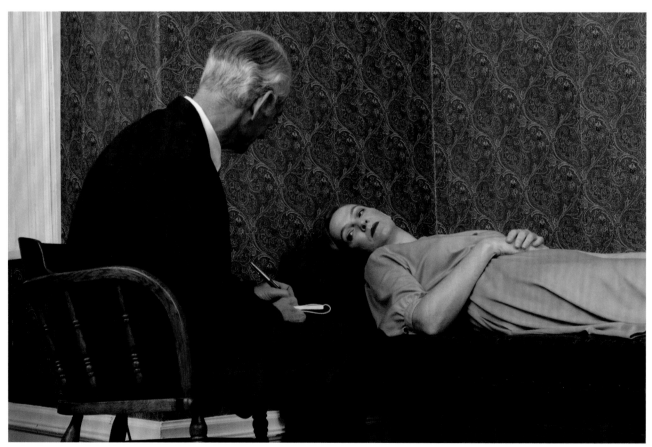

The psychiatrist and his patient. In early photographs of psychiatrists the patients are almost always women.

QUESTIONS FROM 'TEACHING NOTES'

A selection from questions devised by the American experimental artist, Paul Thek, for his students, c.1980. They reflect his belief that creativity is deeply connected to every aspect of an artist's personality, particularly those related to love, sex and close personal relations, as well as the feeling for beauty. 'Every human being', said Joseph Beuys, 'is an artist.' Introspection is a doorway to artistic creation.

What are your requirements in a friend? lover? mate?

What do you do on a date?

What is the purpose of dating?

Do you believe in premarital sex?

What is the main source of difficulty between you and your parents? teachers? friends?

Who are your role models?

Who is the person closest to you at the moment?

Who is the person physically closest to you at the moment?

What in your life is your greatest source of pleasure?

How do you know you love someone?

How do you know that someone is interested in you?

How do you know that you are happy, sad, nervous, bored?

What would it be like if you behaved with absolute power?

What is the most beautiful thing in the world?

What is the purpose of art?

What does 'spiritual' mean to you?

What is the most difficult thing in life for you?

What is the surest way to happiness?

What is attractive in a woman? A man?

Why are you here?

What do you think has been the greatest hurt, both mental and physical, that you have suffered?

What do you think are the qualities of a life fully lived?

What do you do to make yourself more attractive sexually? Why do you do this?

HOW ANGRY ARE YOU?

BY PATRICIA DUNCKER

All the domestic and professional incidents or scenarios described in this questionnaire are authentic.

1. Your TV satellite box has broken down repeatedly. You ring the service support line. They suggest that you go through the entire self-help repair procedure yet again. This method has not worked on three previous occasions. Do you

a) swear violently at the support engineer and threaten her/him?
b) tell your wife/husband/partner/significant other to come downstairs and deal with it?
c) slam down the phone, rip the box free of its leads and hurl it out of your living room window?

2. Your neighbour's gigantic evergreen hedge is darkening your house and garden. He refuses to cut it back. Do you

a) invite him round, point out your lack of light and offer to pay half the costs of lowering the hedge?
b) hack it down yourself at dead of night and pile the cuttings up against his front door?
c) set fire to his entire garden?

3. You are a careful driver. You come to a halt in a line of traffic. The driver behind fails to stop and runs into the back of your car, causing substantial damage. Do you

a) call the police and ask for the other driver's insurance details?
b) burst into tears and splutter out the fact that it is your partner's car, and that she or he will never forgive you?
c) stab the other driver?

4. You sense that you are being edged out at work. Your colleagues fall silent when you approach them, or deliberately change the subject of their discussions. Do you

a) ask your union for advice and seek a meeting with senior management?
b) hack into their e-mails, discover the truth, confirm your suspicions and then send them anonymous death threats?
c) hire the frighteners, and send them round to your colleagues' home addresses?

5. You come home unexpectedly and find your life partner in bed with someone you don't know who is (i) of the same sex as your partner, (ii) of a different sex to you, or (iii) clearly well over twenty years younger than you and your partner. Do you

a) close the door quietly and slip out of the house?
b) begin screaming and refuse to stop?
c) strip off all your clothes, leap into bed and insist on having violent sex with both of them?

6. Your dangerous neighbour has strangled your cat, nailed its body spread-eagled to your door and left you a message warning you to keep your animals off his land. Do you

a) call the police and report the incident?
b) kill his cat with a well-placed poisoned rat?
c) hunt him down with a gun?

Note down your choices (1a, 2b, etc.), then turn to page 186.

Unknown film still, USA, c.1932.

A psychologist and his patient, USA, c.1960.

DREAM AWARENESS SURVEY (DAS)

BY DEREK LINZEY

'Until you make the unconscious conscious, it will direct your life and you will call it fate.' Carl Jung

How in touch are you with your nocturnal self?

Dreams can tell us much about our waking lives. Read the following dream summaries and chose the interpretation you feel is most likely (a, b or c).

1. You dream you are soaring with ease over the countryside.

a) You are in danger of suffering from delusions of grandeur.
b) You should take up hang gliding.
c) Life is going well for you.

2. You dream that you are a student. In this dream you discover you are unprepared for a test. This causes you great anxiety.

a) You should not pursue a teaching career.
b) You are worried about an ongoing or upcoming event or situation in your life.
c) You are nervous about the judgement of others.

3. In your dream you discover that a sleeping bear is under your bed. You are terrified of waking the bear.

a) You are wary of awakening a powerful inner force.
b) You suffer from ursaphobia.
c) You have grievously neglected the housework and need to vacuum under the bed.

4. You are a man and in your dream you are wrestling with a woman.

a) You need to buy a bigger bed for you and your wife.
b) You must come to a better male/female balance within yourself.
c) You might consider a sex change.

5. You dream you are on the tube. You attempt to exit the train but are prevented from doing so.

a) Your life is out of your control.
b) You are uneasy about travelling to unfamiliar places.
c) You should commute by bike.

Now turn to page 186.

DIGITAL DEPENDENCY INDEX (DDI)

BY DEREK LINZEY

'It's supposed to be automatic, but actually you have to push this button.' From John Brunner, *Stand on Zanzibar,* 1968

We live in an increasingly digital world. Just how dependent on your devices have you become? Take the following questionnaire; you might be surprised by what you discover.

If you are or were to become single how do/would you meet other single people?

1. By striking up conversations in museum gift shops or at social gatherings.
2. By responding to ads in the dating section of newspapers.
3. By using an online dating service.
4. By using a location-based dating and social discovery application on your smartphone.

How do you navigate an unfamiliar part of town?

1. By relying on your husband/wife's infallible sense of direction.
2. By consulting a paper map.
3. By using the GPS system (Matilda) in your car.
4. By using the map application on your smartphone.

What is your preferred method to communicate some personal news with friends and relatives?

1. In person over a cup of tea or a gin and tonic.
2. By letter writing.
3. By telephone.
4. By limiting yourself to 140 characters or posting to your instagram.

How do you maintain or keep track of your fitness levels?

1. Through your bi-annual visits to the tailor.
2. By checking the bathroom scale.
3. By monitoring the number of steps you've taken on your device of choice.
4. By obeying your smartwatch's command to stand up every hour.

In case of a fire in which order do you reach for the following? (choose one)

1. Child, husband/wife, pet, phone
2. Child, husband/wife, phone, pet
3. Child, phone, husband/wife, pet
4. Phone, child, husband/wife, pet

Now add up the numbers you have chosen to arrive at your DDS (Digital Dependence Score) and turn to page 186.

EGO HEALTH CHECKUP (EHC)

BY DEREK LINZEY

'My life is short. I can't listen to banality.' V. S. Naipaul

A properly balanced ego is crucial to good mental health. To determine the health of your own ego answer the following questions (as honestly as you can).

When someone pays you a compliment do you

1. Nod and take it as just dues?
2. Blush and accept the compliment?
3. Look behind you to spot the person for whom (surely) the compliment is intended?
4. Scrutinise the complimenter for ulterior motives?

When you look in the mirror, what do you see?

1. The man/woman of your dreams.
2. A flawed but attractively human face.
3. A fat, hairy stranger.
4. Mirrors have been banished from your house.

What is your attitude toward clothes?

1. You live in a naturist community – clothes only hide the glory of your body.
2. Clothes are important to you – they are a considered outward representation of your inner self.
3. You feel comfortable in whatever you wear.
4. Clothes protect the world from the hideousness of your naked form.

In the changing rooms at the pool do you

1. Shower naked whilst conducting an involved routine of stretches?
2. Shower naked but quickly?
3. Shower with your bathing suit on?
4. Skip the shower altogether and quickly dress in one of the private stalls?

When a friend returns the first draft of your manuscript with many considered comments do you

1. Ignore all input – genius is destined to be misunderstood.
2. Consider these comments carefully and incorporate the salient ones into your next draft.
3. You do not share your writing – the mere act of writing is pleasure enough for you.
4. Give up and never write again.

Note down the number of your response to each question, add the numbers together, then turn to page 187.

Tina Mackenzie, psychotherapist, from the series *Head Space, Photographs of Therapeutic Environments*, 2003, by Nick Cunard.

6

FURTHER TESTS

WORD ASSOCIATION TEST

This test is closely associated with Carl Jung, who developed it at the beginning of the last century. (His famous lecture 'The Association Method' was published in 1910.) A list of words of different types (nouns, verbs, adjectives, abstract, concrete, etc.) is read out to the person being tested who, after each word, responds as quickly as possible with the first word that occurs to him or her. The analyst notes the speed and intensity of reactions to the different words, and draws inferences about the underlying reasons for different responses. Responses are also analysed by type (these 'types' differ from clinician to clinician): e.g. opposites (dark/light); associations (night/dream); definitions (table/furniture); predicates, in which the response signals a judgment (knife/dangerous, flower/pretty). These types of response are collated and related to response times, and patterns and recurrences are noted and analysed. The following is Jung's own list, as published in the 1910 lecture.

Many 'associations' are not, of course, purely a function of the individual mind, but simply reflect the frequent co-occurrence of the words in the language environment, e.g. cross/road, left/right, top/class.

1. head	18. sick	35. mountain	52. to part	69. part	86. false
2. green	19. pride	36. to die	53. hunger	70. old	87. anxiety
3. water	20. to cook	37. salt	54. white	71. flower	88. to kiss
4. to sing	21. ink	38. new	55. child	72. to beat	89. bride
5. dead	22. angry	39. custom	56. to take care	73. box	90. pure
6. long	23. needle	40. to pray	57. lead pencil	74. wild	91. door
7. ship	24. to swim	41. money	58. sad	75. family	92. to choose
8. to pay	25. voyage	42. foolish	59. plum	76. to wish	93. hay
9. window	26. blue	43. pamphlet	60. to marry	77. cow	94. contented
10. friendly	27. lamp	44. despise	61. house	78. friend	95. ridicule
11. to cook	28. to sin	45. finger	62. dear	79. luck	96. to sleep
12. to ask	29. bread	46. expensive	63. glass	80. lie	97. month
13. cold	30. rich	47. bird	64. to quarrel	81. deportment	98. nice
14. stem	31. tree	48. to fall	65. fur	82. narrow	99. woman
15. to dance	32. to prick	49. book	66. big	83. brother	100. to abuse
16. village	33. pity	50. unjust	67. carrot	84. to fear	
17. lake	34. yellow	51. frog	68. to paint	85. stork	

Carl Jung. Photographer and date unknown.

SENTENCE COMPLETION TEST

This projective test requires subjects to complete the following sentences in a way that has some meaning for them. Of course this instruction will not necessarily elicit a truthful completion, and some question beginnings are wide open to fantastic and fabricated completions. Who would know if the completed sentence reflects conscious or unconscious thoughts and feelings? How could they know, one way or the other? What do you make of your own efforts?

Invited to a fancy dress party, I would go as ....

The last time I cried was ....

On occasion my nerves ....

In the middle of the night I sometimes ....

Everyone agrees that my father ....

When I was in my teens I thought that at the age I am now I would be ....

My only bad habit is ....

I get upset when ....

I secretly ....

My mother ....

Something I miss about being a child is ....

The last time I said 'sorry' and really meant it was ....

I am paralyzed by fear when ....

Compared with most families mine ....

My idea of a perfect woman ....

In the company of someone much cleverer than me ....

One thing (apart from money) that would improve my life is ....

When I think no-one's looking I sometimes ....

If my father would only ....

I only lose control when ....

If my mother would only ....

If I could travel back in time, I would go to ....

I think most men ....

WHAT WOULD BE THE TITLE OF YOUR AUTOBIOGRAPHY?

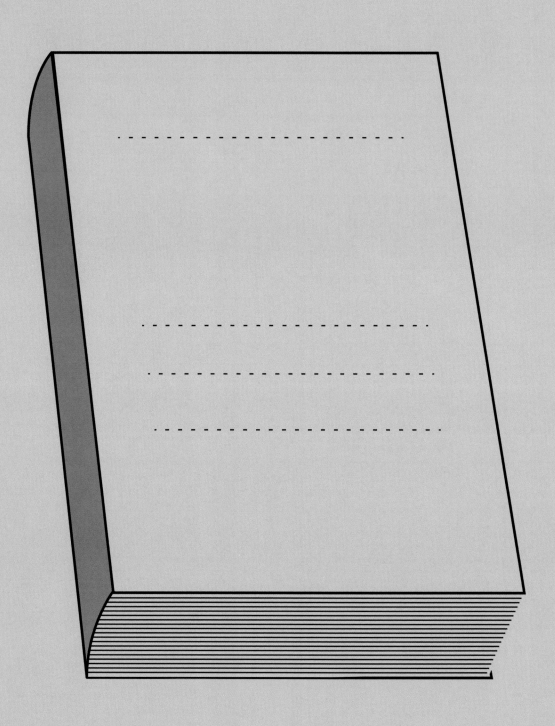

THE COLOUR TEST

A famous colour test was devised by the Swiss psychologist Max Lüscher and first published in 1947. Simple in application, its sophistication lies in its careful matching of attributes not only to the colours preferred by the viewer but to those colours less liked, those towards which he or she feels merely neutral, and those actively disliked. Analysis of the accumulated data, it is claimed, provides the professional tester with a complex psychological profile of the person tested, with clues to will-power, commitment and motivation, emotional and mental conditions, interpersonal skills and aspirations, and much else. The analytic guidelines provided for the test are intriguingly diverse (and sometimes confused) in their categories. Someone who likes brown best, for example, 'wishes to charm, attract and enchant' others, while someone who is neutral about green is 'a friendly person, who bonds easily and could take pleasure in eroticism'.

(That equivocal 'could' is interesting: it is possible, it seems, to be neutral about green and yet not to take pleasure in the erotic.) Actively disliking purple means, according to the test, that you 'want to experience all life has to offer without having to suffer from nervous exhaustion'. (Might it not be the case that those who really like purple might also have a keen appetite for life, and a desire to stay lively?) The interpretations in this book are greatly simplified adaptations, and this generalising approach leaves out of consideration many of the subtleties of the test as administered by professional experts. The test has many applications, having been used, for example, in selection procedures for job candidates and as the basis of industrial interior decor intended to increase productivity. Its efficacy in these various circumstances is difficult to evaluate. The language of the test key has at times a remarkable similarity to that of horoscopes.

From the colour test devised for this book on the next two pages, choose the colours that you actively like, those you feel neutral about and those you actively dislike. Then turn to page 187 for interpretations.

VIOLIN

DOUBLE BASS

PIANO

DRUM

ACCORDION

SAXOPHONE

TRIANGLE

FLUTE

BAGPIPES

7

RELATIONSHIP TESTS

THE FAMILY RELATIONSHIP TEST

Which of the twelve drawings that follow seem to represent the essence of your relationship to your family? These images may help you to identify the optimum passage through notoriously turbulent seas.

Drawings by Adam Dant.

After making your selection, turn to page 188.

7

8

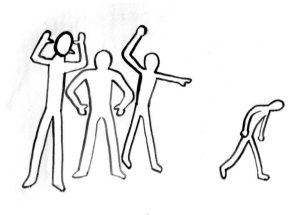

9

10

11

12

THE RELATIONSHIP TEST

Which is the most important relationship in your life?

The thirty-one drawings that follow reveal different dynamics that may be at work. The situations depicted may seem extreme, but perhaps there are elements that you recognise in your own relationship?

Turn to page 188 to discover what your choice may signify.

1

2

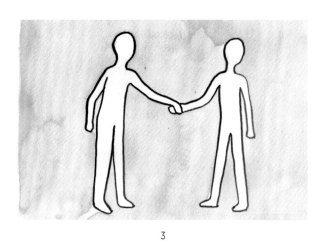

3

4

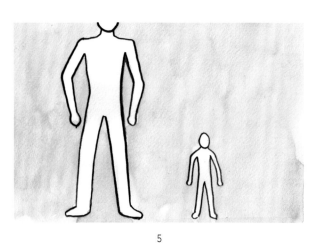

5

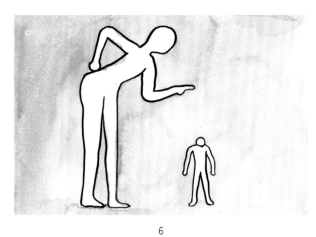

6

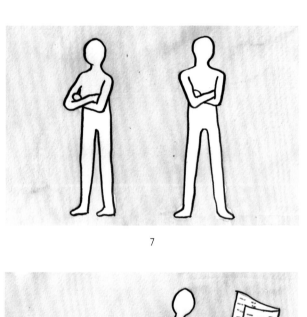

7

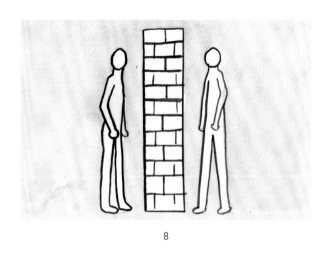

8

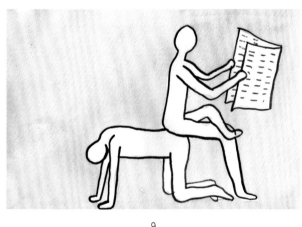

9

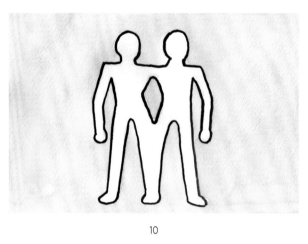

10

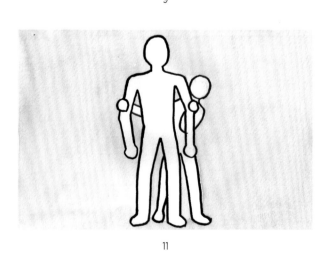

11

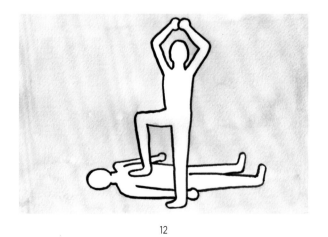

12

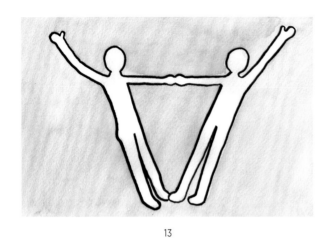

13

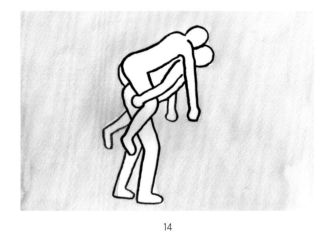

14

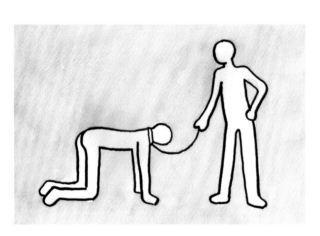

15

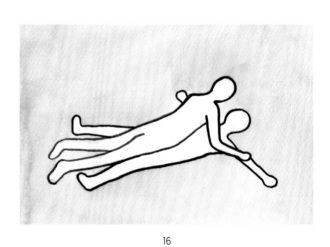

16

17

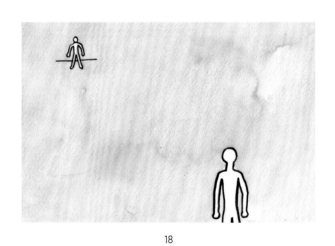

18

19

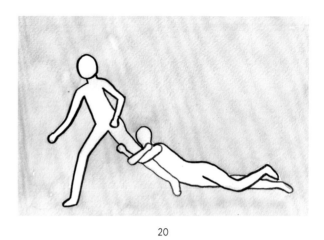

20

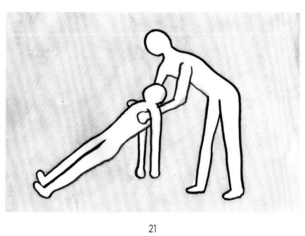

21

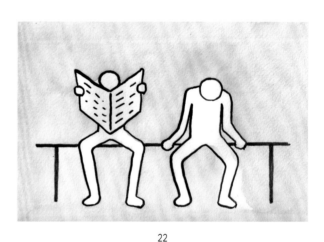

22

23

24

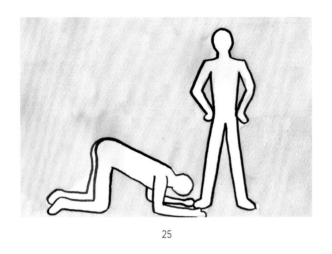

25

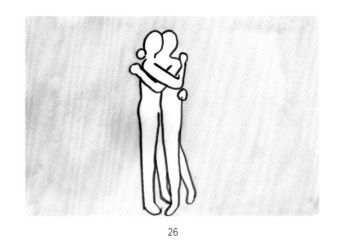

26

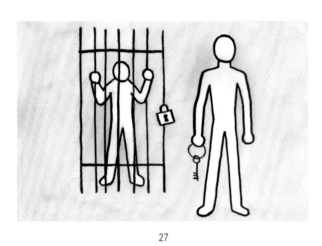

27

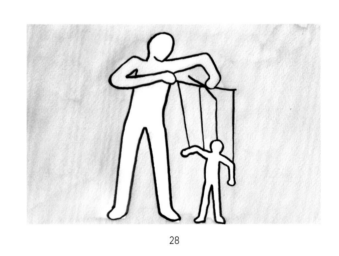

28

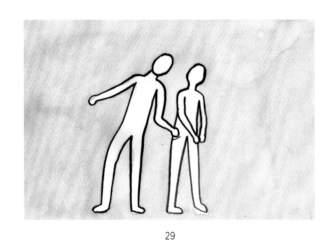

29

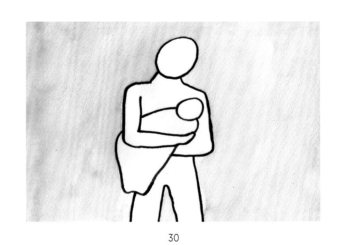

30

8

DRAWING COMPLETION TESTS

THE HOUSE-TREE-PERSON TEST

This is a version of a well-known projective test which was originally confined to the drawing of the human figure. It was based on the assumption that aspects of personality inaccessible in a verbal interview are revealed by the non-verbal activity of drawing. Analysis depends entirely on the subjective response of the clinician. Unlike other projective tests, such as the TAT, the Rorschach and the Drawing Completion Tests, the H-T-P starts with a blank sheet, and provides no prompts beyond the one-word title of the potential drawing. In the clinical situation two types

of analysis might be considered. The first is intrasubjective, i.e. it is confined to what the drawing might reveal about the subject doing the test, and will be augmented by verbal interview. The second is comparative: this will compare features of the drawings that recur across sets of drawings by many subjects, and consider the individual subject's response in relation to codified types of response to the test.

For commentaries turn to page 188.

A somewhat fraught and complex response!

HOUSE

TREE   PERSON

On a sheet of paper make a drawing appropriate to the word in each rectangle.

DRAWING COMPLETION TEST 1

Copy these diagrams onto a sheet of paper.

Draw a picture in each of the six divisions of the diagram opposite, incorporating the lines and shapes already there in five of them. In the blank space numbered 2 draw anything you like.

These tests were devised by the psychiatrist Ehrig Wartegg in 1934 to reveal aspects of personality.

Turn to page 188 for interpretation.

DRAWING COMPLETION TESTS 2 AND 3

As for the previous test, draw a picture in each section opposite, and in those on page 168, incorporating the lines and shapes already there.

Turn to page 189 for interpretation.

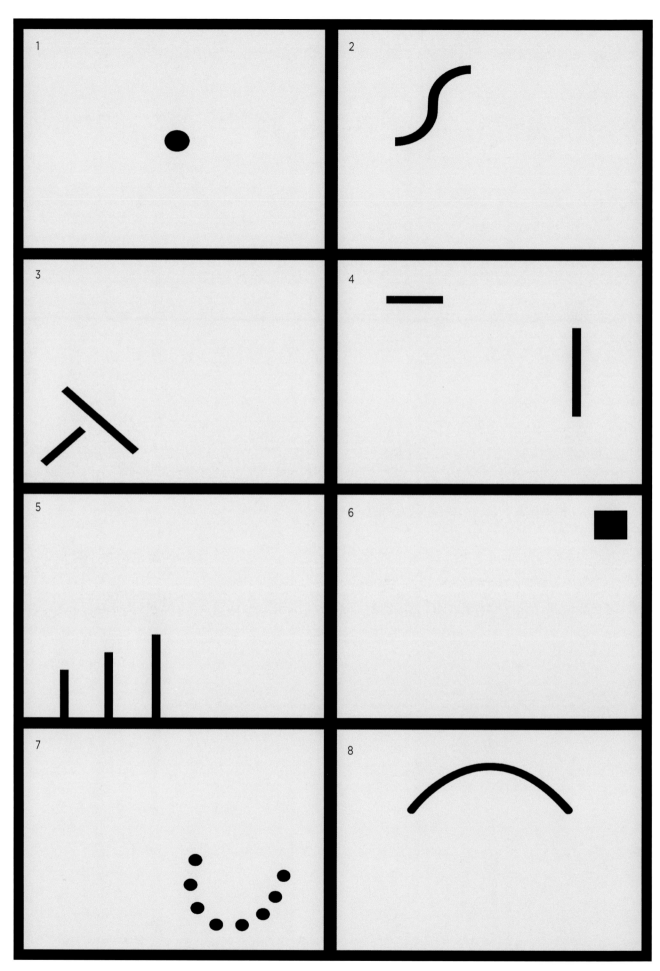

Turn to page 189 for interpretation.

168

9

THE ABSTRACT IMAGE TEST

THE ABSTRACT IMAGE TEST

Psychologists, most notably Hermann Rorschach, have long acknowledged that the associations prompted by certain abstract images might be revelatory of unconscious impulses and emotional or psychological tendencies. Such images may bring to mind aspects of time and space, suggest figures or objects in a fantasy, or invite speculation about any number of dreamlike narratives or scenarios and their interpretations. We may also respond to the purely abstract aspects of an image or an object: its shape or colour, and whether it is bright or dull, hard or soft, jagged or smooth, precise or vague, etc. These components of sensory experience affect all of us in different ways. Why do certain abstract qualities please us, and others not? What kinds of pleasure (or displeasure) do they generate? What do our responses tell us about ourselves?

When we look at an abstract image, several things are likely to occur. We may find resemblances to things we know: we see a disc or a circle as the moon or the sun, a billowing shape as a sail, a cloud or a whale. We may find ourselves making involuntary associations and recollections: we think that reminds us of an event, a place we have visited, a person we know, love or hate, a complex of ideas, or anything else. We ask ourselves what the image 'means', which entails imagination, invention and projection. What we come up with will inevitably in some way reflect our personality, our ways of thinking and feeling about the world, and our unconscious desires and antipathies. What an image 'means' is really what we make it mean.

We all experience those Proustian moments when something commonplace brings back vivid memories from lost time. We are fascinated by the way we associate one thing with another, quite different thing. Association and resemblance breed metaphor, and metaphor is the poetry of our waking lives and a clue to our dreams. Psychologists are interested in these recollections, associations, speculations and inventions. They may provide clues to underlying emotional conditions or neurotic preoccupations, or to suppressed thoughts or emotions; and professional analysis may yield evidence towards the diagnosis of a particular anxiety or neurosis.

Abstract images make an open-ended invitation to the viewer, which partly explains the widespread appeal of abstract art in an age when psychology has come to place such emphasis on the individual personality and its expression. In all human cultures abstract and symbolic images have represented aspects of psychic being and inner feeling: we recognise such images as having significance for our own everyday lives. Ambiguity, the capacity of an image or action to suggest more than one thing at a time, or to propose several meanings simultaneously, indisputably provides one of the great pleasures of art and literature. But some people hate uncertainty and seek unambiguous certainty: it's a matter of temperament, which is to say, of psychological predisposition. Some images move us deeply, we know not why. Some leave us cold.

Contemplate the images on the following pages and then turn to the relevant page for commentaries.

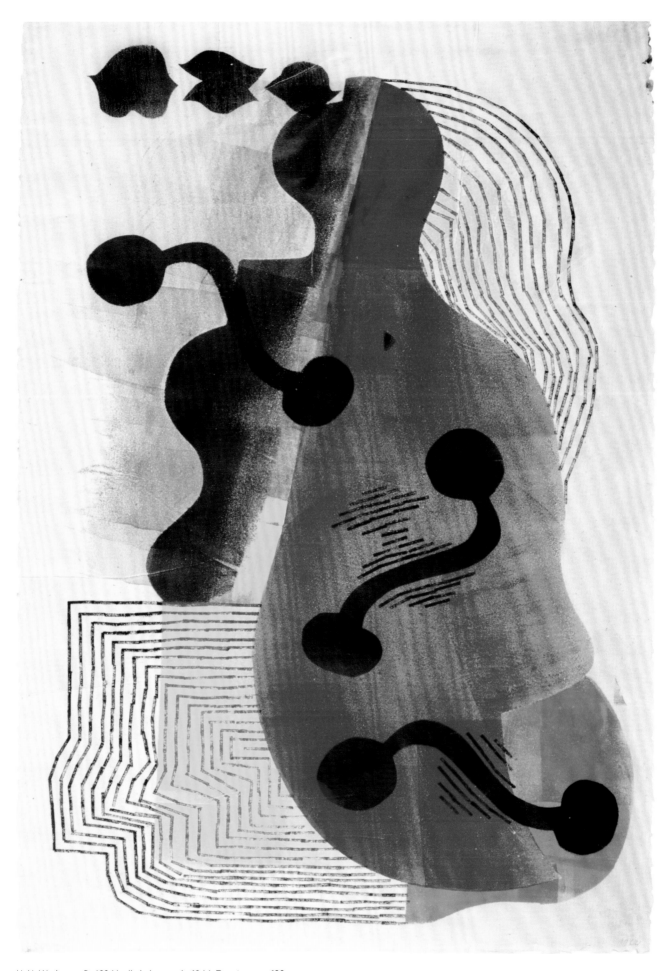

H. N. Werkman, *D-462 Muzikale impressie*, 1944. Turn to page 189.

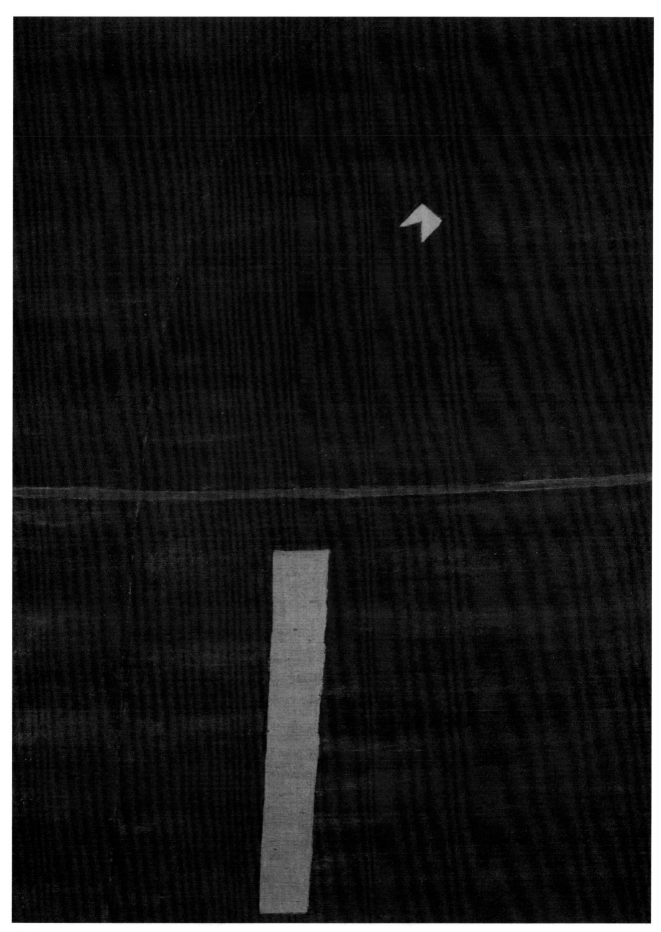

Alfredo Volpi, *Composition,* c.1960-70. Turn to page 189.

Uta Uta Tjangala, *Ceremonial Hat with Special Motifs,* 1971. Turn to page 189.

Tantric painting from Rajasthan, India, c.1963. Turn to page 190.

Sigmar Polke, *Thought Circle*, 1974. Turn to page 190.

Serge Charchoune, *Painted Film Based on a Folk Song*, 1917. Turn to page 190.

PAGE 66

(Whole image) *Aerial view of a roast chicken*
Like anyone, you can have doubts about what you're doing, but essentially you feel very centred and clear about what you need. Alienation is not your thing; passionate engagement is. Speculation about the meaning of life bores you. As Chekhov said, 'That is like asking, 'What is a carrot?' A carrot is a carrot, and nothing more is known about it.'

(Whole image) *A screaming, slightly cartoonish cat that has seen something shocking*
You like to get stuck in and work things out as they come up, hence your loud, tempestuous side. It is very important for you to be listened to, to feel someone is on your side. Negotiation and conflict are facts of life as far as you're concerned, so although you are not abrasive at heart, you can come across that way. You can sometimes remind people of the old joke: How many New York cab drivers does it take to change a lightbulb? What's it to ya?

(Upside down) *Someone in a wig, a judge or a faceless woman*
You set yourself high standards and expect others to do the same. You're unconvinced that patience is a virtue. As Picasso said, 'You do it first, then someone else does it pretty.'

(Upside down) *A woman has clubbed her husband to death with a pair of frozen hams*
Like the Neapolitans, you think, '*Un amore non è bello, se non che la fizzaricello*' (Love's no good unless some sparks fly).' All the fun is in the kissing and making up, although you try not to go to sleep on an argument.

(Whole image) *Someone's jaws being approached by the forceps of a sinister doctor*
Life isn't meant to be easy, and people can't always be expected to get along. You feel you just have to be yourself and if people can't handle that, well, as they say in Barbados, 'The eggshell have no right at the hard rock dance.'

(White space inside image) *A rocket or tower, specifically the dark tower of Sauron in* Lord of the Rings
You work extremely hard, constantly setting yourself new challenges in an attempt to become stronger. You get a lot done and are highly appreciated professionally. The message in your private life may be that you need to lighten up and not be so controlling. You file this neatly in your 'To Do' folder.

PAGE 67

(Whole image) *A strong man, flexing his muscles*
You are highly capable, to put it mildly. Running marathons, reconditioning bicycles, cultivating new strains of plants, raising money for social causes – you master everything you turn your hand to. Like a competitive athlete, you are naturally gifted and extremely determined. Having the bar raised is a familiar experience, and you pride yourself on always being equal to the challenge.

(Top of image) *A pair of rams at the top, butting with heads lowered*
You're self-disciplined, reliable, good at seizing the initiative, and, in general, a whirlwind of activity. You always come across as very certain about what you're doing, which inspires confidence in clients and work colleagues, despite your suffering from raw nerves. When you're feeling threatened or under pressure, you can feel very stressed, but only those close to you tend to notice.

(Whole image) *A scorpion*
You are highly tuned, like a gymnast or ballerina. Things like diet and sleep can be issues, since you are physically very sensitive. Sometimes you wonder whether there's a connection between this and how you feel about yourself, your self-worth, but anything that smacks of therapy tends to get on your nerves.

(Whole image) *A lobster, shrimp, langoustine*
A romantic at heart, you nevertheless have quite a lot of defences in place. You work so hard and life can be such a struggle that you sometimes wonder if you can sacrifice your peace of mind for the unpredictability of a relationship. Someone can innocently, unthinkingly, mess up the order you've created, and you can become completely discouraged. The whole notion of kindred spirits suddenly seems a joke.

(Whole image) *Fallopian tubes*
You have a sense of stalled potential, of putting an enormous amount into life and yet still waiting for it to start. Your idea of how things should be – who you should be with, what you should be doing, etc. – is very vivid, and if reality falls short of expectations, your considerable achievements provide little consolation. A philosophical approach such as Rimbaud's '*Ô saisons, ô châteaux, quelle âme est sans défauts?*' ('Oh seasons, oh castles, what soul is without blemish?'), strikes you as trite at best.

PAGE 68

(Centre of image) *Two figures leaning forward – monkeys, courtiers or spiritual devotees of some sort bowed in prayer*
(Whole image, including white space) *Person praying*
A cerebral soul, you have a great capacity for imaginative, rigorous thought. You know all too well the concentration and patience required to do anything good, and can't see why anyone would settle for anything less if they care about what they're doing. You want to feel like the New Orleans piano player Allen Toussaint, who said of his mentor Professor Longhair 'A rule breaker is a rule maker. He blew my socks off, and I haven't worn any since.'

(Whole image) *Racing car, speed, voluptuousness*
(Centre of image) *Two furry little cubs, babies, devils*
Your highly developed imagination is one of the first things people notice about you. 'Metaphorical' is your instinctive mode. You excel at constructing other worlds, seeing things from other people's points of view, imagining yourself soaring to great heights or plummeting to your doom.

(Whole image) *Dentist's/barber's chair*
You are sensitive and generous, a combination that ensures you get a lot out of life and take it painfully to heart in equal measure. Given the transparency of your feelings, people often want to look after you, which can occasionally confuse your understanding of intimacy. Very formal, conventional environments drain you. You would not thrive in the New England setting the artist Cy Twombly grew up in: 'Once I said to my mother, "You would be happy if I just kept well-dressed and [had] good manners," and she said "What else is there?" '

(Upside down) *A woman lying back with her legs open*
You can get very distracted. Within moments you can go from being completely in the present to looking down on it from a huge height, analyzing it to within an inch of its life. Balance is crucial for you, being able to stay in touch with your physical, sensual side. Life is about sensations as well as thoughts; it is about the texture of concrete particulars, the smell of the Paris Metro or what it feels like to hold a mouse in your hand, as Iris Murdoch once put it.

(Whole image) *Two dark forces or figures, perhaps female, about to invade and consume a prone figure/torso*
You may progress as you digress, to paraphrase Tristram Shandy, or you may just digress. How many unfinished letters or emails, unmade phone calls trail in your wake? As Philip Roth said, 'The road to hell is paved with works-in-progress.'

PAGE 69

(Whole image) *Beetle, scarab, possibly with crab's claws*
You are very hardworking, good at handling your career and the 'game' in general. Success comes naturally to you. You arrange your pieces on the board, lay your plans and follow them through. You can be careful or daring as the situation requires. In the end, you know it's always the cleverest or luckiest play that prevails.

(Whole image, except bottom centre) *Pair of emus facing one another, wearing feather boas, dancing on stage at the Moulin Rouge*
You feel the pull of glamour and the high-life like gravity. You unfailingly know the place to be and enjoy being there, although sometimes you don't like how you feel the next day, or what you see in the mirror as you head for the dance floor. At times you wonder why this is; at others you tell yourself not to take yourself so seriously.

(Either side of image) *Two pairs of hummingbirds, wings beating*
You're a connoisseur, a *beija-flor* (kisser of flowers) as the Portuguese call the hummingbird. Just as hummingbirds sometimes feed on as many as one thousand flowers a day, you are constantly on the move, pursuing objects of desire, seeking out beautiful things.

(Bottom of image) *Sunglasses or bra, beard*
You like dressing up and it suits you, although you can worry excessively about what people think of you and seek external solutions – a new car, new clothes – to internal problems. You are tempted to rationalise this as a Warholian creed – life is just surfaces – but you're not sure whether this solves everything.

(Whole image) *Skeleton* (details) *Bones*
Life can seem like a treadmill or a merry-go-round repeating itself over and over. You worry about feeling drained and hollow, grinding to a halt. Sometimes you think you should take more emotional risks.

(Whole image) *Flying thing with eyes or an alien figure with stubby feet and no centre or bikini-wearing goddess with unnerving face*
No-one could be a more dependable friend when it comes to the crunch, but you can appear flighty in the day-to-day. You get huge satisfaction from getting in touch with friends you haven't talked to for a while, a satisfaction that is mutual.

PAGE 70

(Whole image) *Pansies, with attendant connotations of spring; bird of paradise*

The wind is in your sails, a state of affairs that tends to emphasise your charming, energising qualities. You believe in discussion, want to learn from others, are attentive, modest and thoughtful, and like people as a rule. This broad philanthropy may reflect itself either in a strain of non-conformism – the sense that individuals should be free to do whatever they want – or in something more political.

(Whole image) *Pressed flowers of various sorts, including orchids, irises and cyclamen*

You are very aware of what it's like to have been the object of a lot of attention as a child. The jury is out as to whether this is a good thing; sometimes you think you may have overly high expectations of yourself. You are not seriously worried about being your own worst enemy, but you can understand what Degas meant when he said, 'There is a kind of success that is indistinguishable from panic.'

(Whole image) *Moth, butterfly with sting in tail*

Your affable, sociable exterior may not prepare people for how independent you are, the doggedness with which you revolve in your own, unique orbit. Naturally you're drawn to the limelight – in many ways, it's where your talents mean you belong – but you're dubious about the costs, and, even more than that, you can't stand anyone telling you what to do. You are profoundly unbiddable; at the first hint of coercion, you disappear.

(Whole image) *Eyes in darkness, with blinkers on*

You have a great capacity for introspection. You go somewhere inside yourself far out of others' reach, and think things over exhaustively. This is not always easy for other people. As Spencer Tracy says to Rosalind Russell in *His Girl Friday* after she divorces him, 'I wish you hadn't done that, Hildy. . . Divorce me. Makes a fellow lose all faith in himself. . . Almost gives him a feeling he wasn't wanted.'

THE STORY TEST
PAGE 98

1. The Forest

If you imagined the forest as dark and threatening this is indicative of your attitude towards the journey you are on at this moment in your life. Alternatively, seeing light would suggest you are an optimist at heart, perhaps even naïvely so. If you saw a path in the forest, this suggests you are still finding your way in life, things are not yet settled. Those who feel more secure or sure of their development tend not to see a path.

2. The Cup

The cup symbolises wealth and your attitude towards it. Did you imagine a trophy or a cup of coffee? You were given an opportunity to reward yourself and see something of value, did you do this?

If you left the cup alone, this means you chose to ignore a reward. Either material wealth has little real value to you or you didn't think you had worked hard enough for it!

Did you pick the cup up and drink from it? This means you found a practical use for it, taking a 'here and now' attitude towards the reward.

Taking the cup with you on your journey means you saw it as something of value. You are quick to reward yourself and generally seek out new opportunities.

3. Water

The water here represents your attitudes towards sex and desire.

The speed at which you saw the water moving indicates your sexual appetite, but not necessarily your need. The faster the water, the greater your appetite.

The depth indicates what you expect from sex to feel fulfilled: seeing shallow water suggests you enjoy deep and intense love-making whereas seeing fast-moving water means 'little and often' is enough for you.

The more easily you crossed the water, the more comfortable or liberal you are likely to be in your approach to sex. So a difficult crossing suggests an unease or neurosis attached to your sexuality.

4. The Bear

The bear represents problems in your life and how you cope with them. Did you jump at the chance to see a problem? If you saw a teddy bear then one would assume your life is relativity stress free! You glide through life with ease.

However most people will see a real bear. If the bear hasn't noticed you, or has but is minding its own business, then this indicates that the problems in your life are manageable. Your stresses are not too big to handle. Given the chance to see a big problem, you chose not to.

If, however, you chose to see a dangerous animal, a threat to your safety in some way, you are likely to be under high levels of stress or worry in your real life – perhaps you need a holiday?

How you get around the bear is indicative of how you deal with and resolve problems. Most people are able to summon up the courage and placate the bear long enough to move past the threat.

5. The Beach
The image of the beach symbolises how you relate to others. The number of people you pictured on the beach relates directly to the amount of human contact you want in your life. A social extrovert is most comfortable in the company of lots of people and will seek out this 'audience' wherever he or she travels. Likewise, those that see a deserted beach are usually happy to spend long periods in their own company.

Where on the beach you saw the people is also significant. If they were very close this suggests you crave contact with other people most of the time. If they were sitting in the distance then you are likely to feel happier to know someone is there for you, but without the proximity – you are content to have your own space.

THE FEELING TEST
PAGE 100

The Shopping Mall PAGE 102
1) Fragile 2) Excited 3) Insecure 4) Helpless 5) Happy
6) Onlooker 7) Triumphant 8) Praising 9) Contemplating
10) Celebrating 11) United 12) Confident 13) Carefree 14) Seeker
15) Rebuffed 16) Helper 17) Risk-taker 18) Upset 19) and 20)
United 21) Lonely 22) Mischievous 23) Help! 24) Frustrated
25) Excluded 26) Tantrum 27) Unique 28) Overloaded
29) Oblivious 30) Clumsy 31) Fun-loving 32) Playful 33) Follower
34) Hurt 35) Target 36) Passive 37) and 38) Secure 39) Cautious
40) Overwhelmed 41) Escapist 42) Misunderstood 43) Loving
44) Bossy 45) Angry 46) Victim

The House of Personalities PAGE 104
1) Seeker 2) Opportunist 3) Lost 4) Dissatisfied 5) Procrastinator
6) Enabler 7) Helper 8) Keeper 9) Nosy 10) Fulfilled 11) Loving
12) Victim 13) Perfectionist 14) Contained 15) Liberated
16) Untrustworthy 17) Gullible 18) Narcissist 19) Happy
20) Celebratory 21) Cautious 22) Angry 23) Inert 24) Proper
25) Creative 26) Dependable 27) Organiser 28) Insecure
29) Friendly 30) Open 31) Unconscious 32) Parental 33) Anxious
34) Fragile

The Climbing Frame PAGE 105
1) Mischievous 2) Help! 3) Accident-prone 4) In charge
5) Carefree 6) Self-satisfied 7) Vandal 8) Assassin 9) Hanging on
10) Playmate 11) Playmate 12) Ostracised 13) Show-off 14) Happy
15) Elated 16) Helper 17) Sulky 18) Victim 19) Loner
20) Encouraging 21) Follower

THE CB IDENTITY QUESTIONNAIRE (CBIQ)
PAGE 115

Mostly a) Who are you? You appear not to have a clear sense of your own identity. I don't even know who I'm talking to here.
Mostly b) Betwixt and between, as many of us. Confident yet hesitant, open-minded yet needing security, you are prone to tears, which is a likeable trait.
Mostly c) You know exactly who you are. Such certainty worries me.

EVERYDAY GUILT TEST (EGT)
PAGE 119

Answer scale: 16 = excess guilt, 4 = not nearly enough guilt

THE 'MATTER IN THE WRONG PLACE' TEST
PAGE 124

Low scores (1 to 15)
You have the common sense of a country doctor who knows how to live in modest harmony with nature. The concept that Earth has a spirit and a beauty of her own comes naturally to you. Indeed you relish the knowledge that spirit is the inside of things and matter their visible outer aspect. Keep up the good work!

Medium scores (16 to 25)
The majority of people score within this range. On the one hand you are deeply concerned over the loss of connection with nature. You know that nature is the nourishing soil of the soul. Yet you can find yourself distracted by the 'dirt of civilization'. Undecided in this way, you may find that from day to day your score varies.

High scores (26 and above)
Jung's concern was that 'the more successful we become in science and technology, the more diabolical are the uses to which we put our inventions and discoveries.' It could be that you have a very busy life, and that consequently you find you have little time for those who believe that nature is not matter only, she is also spirit. But it would be as well to bear in mind Carl Jung's psychological rule that when an inner situation is not made conscious, it happens outside as fate.

THE SHYNESS QUESTIONNAIRE (TSQ)
PAGE 130

Mostly a) You have nothing to hide (I may be wrong; these questionnaires are not exact) and no worries about what people think of you. In olden times you would have made a good living selling encyclopaedias door-to-door.

Mostly b) The world is a difficult place, but you are doing fine. You've probably worked out that everyone is shy in some degree, and that shyness can take on a mask of arrogance.

HOW ANGRY ARE YOU?
PAGE 136

1. If you scored the following replies: 1c), 2c), 3c), 4b), 5b), 6c) congratulations. You are a very angry person indeed. You make Othello look like a reasonable man. You are decisive, quick to act, implacable and imaginative in your revenge. Bravo.

2. If you answered the question with the following pattern: 1b), 2a), 3a), 4a), 5a), 6a) you are apparently sane and deliberate but also exceedingly sinister. You can control your feelings and give every appearance of being rational, reasonable and judicious. You should seek professional help at once.

3. If neither of the above patterns suits your replies and you chose an inconsistent mixture of options, beware. You have a dangerous streak. You are unpredictable, irrational and mad.

DREAM AWARENESS SURVEY (DAS)
PAGE 139

Not In Touch (NIT)

Somewhat In Touch (SIT)

Very In Touch (VIT)

1. Flying dream
a) VIT. This dream may be your unconscious warning not to overestimate your own powers. No matter how our lives are going, it is important always to keep a foot on the ground. Think Icarus here.
b) NIT. It's unlikely that your dream is urging you to literal flight.
c) SIT. Perhaps life is going well for you and this is merely a reflection of your high spirits – indeed dreams such as these are very pleasant. It is however always advisable to keep one foot on the ground.

2. Student dream
a) NIT. This dream should not dissuade you from a career in the classroom; rarely are dreams so literal.
b) VIT. If you were a nervous student as a child, any number of non-academic related anxieties might now be represented by dreams set in the classroom.
c) SIT. Perhaps, though the specific judgement implied in test taking does not necessarily translate into a more generalised fear of judgement.

3. Sleeping bear
a) VIT. Awakening the beast within. Tiptoeing around a wild (potentially dangerous) animal while it is sleeping is probably a sign that something powerful is brewing inside . . . and wanting to be expressed. Proceed with caution and you might find that this bear's energy can be harnessed for your benefit.
b) SIT. Unlikely. Though you may, in fact, be afraid of bears (perhaps wisely).
c) NIT. Only you and your loved ones know if you are a slob. Such dreams will shed no light on the subject.

4. Wrestling with the opposite sex
a) NIT. While you may indeed need a bigger mattress, this is not the most likely issue with this dream. (More likely your wife will insist on one herself if you've been wrestling with her in the night.)
b) VIT. Dreams often act as correctives to our waking lives. In this case you might want to pay attention to the female side of yourself – she might be saying that she feels under-represented.
c) SIT. Though this dream may indicate a male/female imbalance, it's unlikely that your unconscious self is advising you to pursue such a radical path.

5. Tube dream
a) VIT. Tube trains run on fixed tracks to fixed destinations. That you're not allowed to deviate from this course in this dream might indicate that you feel your fate is beyond your control.
b) SIT. This is a possible interpretation, though the underground train is probably a red herring.
c) NIT. Although cycling is a cheap, healthy mode of transport, this dream is not advising you on modes of transport.

DIGITAL DEPENDENCY INDEX (DDI)
PAGE 140

13 to 20: Digitally Independent (DI): You have somehow managed to steer clear of the trappings of the digital age. This impressive feat was (no doubt) achieved through diligent conscious effort, but might have come at the price of puzzled (and perhaps alienated) friends and family. Behind your back you might be referred to as The Luddite.

30 to 34: Mild Digital Dependency (MDD): You are not in total denial of the modern world. You have probably found a comfortable place for technology in your life, although you might

sometimes be (inadvertently) excluded from social events, and be somewhat confused by everyday conversation and social behaviours.

45 to 48: Borderline Digital Dependency (BDD): Digital technology has assumed an important role in your life. You might find however that you're glancing too often at your screen in company, and that a lengthy power outage might cause unexpected distress. From this position the slide into TDD is shorter than you might think.

56 to 59: Total Digital Dependency (TDD): You are a digital junkie. The digital world (from your perspective) might already have supplanted the physical one. You might want to check if you still have a wife and/or that your friends actually exist. A long, disconnected walk in the park is advisable.

EGO HEALTH CHECKUP (EHC)
PAGE 141

4 to 5: Inflated Ego. Unfortunately you suffer from narcissism. This might explain why you tend to remain single, why your colleagues prefer not to work with you and why people tend to avoid you (and your stimulating anecdotes) at parties. It is advisable that you take a good long look at yourself: not by gazing lovingly into the mirror but by noticing how your behaviour impacts on others.

10 to 13: Healthy Ego. Congratulations! You have achieved a healthy, balanced ego. This means that you are in a position (if you so wish) to your enjoy life with someone else and to benefit professionally from the input of others. You are also able to enjoy a bit of good-humoured ribbing at your own expense.

18 to 20: Deficient Ego. A deficiency in ego is often mistaken for hard-nosed realism or extreme modesty. Really though, in not asserting your own worth, you undermine your ability to function in the world. You deprive yourself and those near you of access to your unique and wonderful qualities. Are you really so unattractive? Is your work really inferior to the next person's? Surely not.

THE COLOUR TEST
PAGE 149

What follows is adapted and reduced from a key to Lüscher's test.

actively like = **L**   neutral = **N**   actively dislike = **D**

Grey: **L** This is the colour of the middle ground: you like to be uncommitted and find quiet acceptance from others. **N** You are a laid-back observer. **D** You like to join groups and try to achieve goals with great energy and enthusiasm.

Black: **L** The colour that says 'No'. You would like to be confident, self-possessed and recognised, but you are in revolt against your fate. **N** You hold your ground to achieve your aims. **D** You are in control of your destiny and are well-grounded, though you may be reluctant to take action to resolve stressful situations.

Yellow: **L** You are happy and positive, like to take dynamic action and achieve results. **N** You approach life with a happy-go-lucky aplomb. You are optimistic and hard-working (most of the time). **D** You may have suffered setbacks and become disappointed. If your hopes and dreams have been dashed you may have become defensive and withdrawn.

Red: **L** You are defined by passion and energy, you are impulsive, ambitious and sexy, You live life to the full. **N** You are hopeful and have great expectation from life, you may want more excitement out of life. **D** Your lust for life has diminished, you may have felt the need to give up fun and games.

Brown: **L** You are likely to be restless and insecure, and yet you wish to charm and be attractive to others. **N** You have a subtle sense of discrimination, and you are not unduly concerned about your health, being probably in good shape; you like to be in a secure and refined atmosphere, with an air of intimacy. **D** You don't care enough about your body, and you may feel stressed because your delicate sensibilities are often offended.

Green: **L** You like the comforts, possessions and good things of life. You are a high achiever and you like impressing others, but you worry about failure. **N** You may have been disappointed by not always getting as much as you desired, and hope for a more sympathetic and amicable environment, perhaps because you are a friendly person who could take pleasure in eroticism. **D** Your ego has been bruised, and you have an unsatisfied desire to mix with others who share your high standards. Unsatisfied with your lot, you may be highly critical of others, sarcastic and stubborn.

Blue: **L** You are calm and loyal but sensitive and easily hurt; you like the good life and contentment, and are agitated if things go badly in that direction. You need a stable relationship. Contented, you are likely to put on weight. **N** You are aware of the finality of fate, and tend to a phlegmatic and sometimes unhappy compromise with your life, even when you long for a definitive resolution. **D** You are discontented and long to be free of the ties that restrict you.

Purple: **L** You are torn between impulsiveness and calm acceptance, between dominance and submissiveness; you tend to the mystical and the magical in relationships, and your emotional immaturity means you get stuck in dreams of wishful thinking and fantasy. You need to avoid excitement: you've had too much already. **N** You can participate with others, so long as not too much is demanded of you; fantasy is so enjoyable that it's hard to grow up. **D** You are mature and can look harsh reality in the face; you want to experience all that life has to offer without suffering from nervous exhaustion.

THE FAMILY RELATIONSHIP TEST
PAGE 154

1. Excluded 2. Commander 3. Time to move on 4. Burdened
5. Escaping 6. Unified 7. The boss 8. Well-balanced 9. Victimised
10. Held back 11. Feeling small 12. Outsider

THE RELATIONSHIP TEST
PAGE 156

1. Celebration 2. Humiliation 3. Tentative 4. Triumphant
5. Superiority 6. Authority 7. Stalemate 8. Blocked
9. Dominated 10. Enmeshed 11. Protective 12. Champion
13. Balanced 14. Supportive 15. Enslaved 16. Submissive
17. Shut out 18. Distant 19. Persecuted 20. Dependency
21. Trusting 22. Remote 23. Escaping 24. Contemplative
25. Subservient 26. Loving 27. Entrapment 28. Manipulated
29. Endearing 30. Caring

HOUSE-TREE-PERSON TEST
PAGE 163

House
1. Notice the size of the house: a small house represents renunciation of family life, while a large house means the person is overwhelmed by his family.
2. Observe the walls of the house: weak lines represent fragility in the ego, while strong lines mean the need to fortify boundaries.
3. Determine the amount of detail put into the roof: the more detail, the more the person concentrates on fantasies, while an incomplete roof means evading formidable ideas.
4. Note the inclusion of windows, doors and pavements, which indicate openness to interacting with other people.
5. Discern the inclusion of bushes, shades, shutters, bars and curtains, which indicate a person's hesitation to open himself or herself to others.

Tree
1. Notice the size of the trunk: a small trunk represents a weak ego, while a large trunk indicates a larger ego.
2. Observe whether the trunk is split in half, which indicates a split personality.

3. Determine what kind of limbs were drawn: detached or small branches represent a difficulty communicating with others, big branches mean connecting with others too much, pointy branches indicate hostility and dead branches represent desolation.
4. Note whether leaves are included: drawing leaves represents successfully connecting with others, while no leaves mean emptiness and detached leaves indicates a lack of nurturing.
5. Discern the details of the roots of the tree: while normal roots represent a grounded person, a lack of roots means instability, exaggerated roots indicate an obsession with examining reality, and dead roots represent feeling completely removed from reality.

Person
1. Notice the position of the arms: open arms represent an inclination to connect with others, closed arms mean hostility and disconnected arms indicate defencelessness.
2. Observe the position of the hands: pointed fingers and balled fists represent hostility, while hidden or gloved hands mean antisocial tendencies.
3. Note the details of the legs and feet: figures cut off at the bottom of the paper represent powerlessness, while both large and small feet mean the need for greater stability.
4. Determine the details of the mouth: an open or large mouth represents dependence, a closed mouth means rejection of needs and a slash mouth or teeth indicate verbal hostility.
5. Discern how detailed the face is: the use of more facial details indicates a person's need to portray himself in an acceptable way.

DRAWING COMPLETION TEST 1
PAGE 165

Box 1. This drawing relates to your sense of self. You may have been assertive or tentative (drawn a face, coloured the circle in, etc.) or you may have suggested that there are pressures from outside the circle of yourself. You may happily have seen yourself as a beaming sun, or a flower.
Box 2. Your whole life is revealed in this space. Oh dear! without prompt or guideline you have revealed your innermost self.
Box 3. The square is an architectural unit; your response here relates to your feelings about your house/home or garden. These may have implications with regard to aspects of your identity.
Box 4. The two lines stand for the inescapable dualisms of the universe, especially the duality of sex. You may have just revealed your deepest feelings about love. (On the other hand, you may not.)
Box 5. This motif has to do with your emotional life. Are you floating on or above the waves, or are you sinking below them? Are you waving or drowning? Or did you see and project something else altogether?
Box 6. This will reveal how you relate to your friends, who are at once part of you and separate from you.

DRAWING COMPLETION TEST 2
PAGE 167

Box 1. How you see yourself.
Box 2. How others see you.
Box 3. Childhood/adolescence.
Box 4. Your romantic life.
Box 5. Your future.
Box 6. Death.

DRAWING COMPLETION TEST 3
PAGE 168

Box 1.   Shows how adaptable you are.
Box 2.   Shows your ability to relate and how affectionate you are.
Box 3.   Shows your motivation and desire to go forward.
Box 4.   Shows your ability to overcome difficulties or problems.
Box 5.   Shows your capacity for taking decisions and acting
            on them.
Box 6.   Shows analytical ability.
Box 7.   Shows your feelings and emotions.
Box 8.   Shows your ability to interact socially.

THE ABSTRACT IMAGE TEST
PAGE 169
MEL GOODING WRITES

PAGE 171
There is something of a figure in this image, but pictured, or experienced, it seems, from within: it is not so much a picture of a body, as what it *feels like* to be in a body, caught up in a complex of sensations and inner feelings. But what sensations, what feelings?

Do you feel that this body is experiencing ecstatic pleasure, as in a dance, perhaps singing wonderful crazy words that turn into leaf and petal shapes about your head, released from the mind and flying free? You are in this case probably an extrovert hedonist, at once a lover of bodily pleasures and a dreamer of psychic freedom: those strangely soft, dumb-bell shapes correspond to internal rhythms of tension release, as mind and body become one sensation of joy.

Or do you find yourself resisting those insistent rhythms represented by the curving, organic, concentric lines around the 'shoulder', and finding a kind of reassurance in control suggested by the angular sharp-cornered, similarly concentric pattern at bottom left? In this reading, the body in the image responds to

this rhythmic counterpoint with a gestural movement, turning now this way, now that way, now this way, down its centre; the passion of the sun-yellow and blushing pink is offset by the grounded vegetable green. You are more grounded as a type, perhaps: you like to keep a balance and avoid extremes.

PAGE 173
Blue is the colour of space, endlessness, infinity. To look into the air above us on a fine day is to be aware of a vastness of a film-like blue without beginning and without end. For some this induces wonder, a reverie of oneness with the heavens. At times others feel a loss of orientation that is dizzying: they suffer a kind of reverse vertigo, a groundless fear of losing touch with the ground beneath their feet. 'All that is solid melts into air.' Blue may thus have more than one effect on the spectator: it can bring calm and restfulness, or memories of fear, and perturbation. (Other colours may have similarly opposing effects.)

Which of these contradictory responses is most like yours? It may be that you may feel both, at different times, depending on the play of your mind, and what lies beneath its surface. For what you feel about this expansive blue may be as much a projection of your *present* feelings as it is reflection of a simple unvarying reaction. If you are in a period of psychic calm, your spirit untroubled, you may find yourself enjoying the sense of cosmic bliss. If you are in some way disturbed (even if you are unaware of it), you may feel disorientated and xenophobic.

The grey upright in the lower half may seem to stand for a figure, maybe you, the spectator: it hasn't quite got its foot on the ground. And that little crown-like shape floating above the line: is it your hat, blown away on a sudden gust? A bird? A kite? Does it induce intimations of loss? It seems to belong to the floating upright figure, but it is up and away, disconnected, lifted away into space, perhaps forever. Some people suffer unease at flying, or even simply watching a kite: it seems to be at the mercy of unpredictable and invisible forces, beyond control. They are caught up in psychic uncertainty, even a kind of simulated panic.

PAGE 175
You may feel that this drawing draws you in, takes you to its centre. It may induce a sense of being centred, protected and embraced by the womb-like configuration of concentric circles. You may feel you have been taken into the heart of things. Such a response suggests a personality that is itself centred, that is content to let the world – and the universe, with its stars, suns and moons – spin around you. You are egocentric and yet in a lively way aware of external contingencies. You like things as they are, and want them to continue to be so.

On the other hand you may see first and foremost that central figure, upright and poised, arms outstretched to embrace the whirling world, full of a pulsating inner energy that engages with the dynamics of things, that reaches out, unperturbed by chaos.

These alternative responses are not necessarily exclusive. The first may be described as feminine (though not female): the second as masculine (though not male). You may feel each of them at different times, and then, in an instant of deep joy, experience both simultaneously. Try it. As they come together you may enjoy a moment in which there is perfect psychic unity, a sense of ecstatic integrity.

PAGE 177

You may see this as a potently emotive image, or as a focus for pure meditation. It is susceptible of many interpretations. It requires a period of intense contemplation: it may at once suggest both fullness and emptiness.

In the first case, you may see the deep blue central ellipse as an image of concentrated dark matter into which all things have been drawn and gathered. The pink watercolour cloud may intimate blood and fire, being absorbed into the perfect oval void, a universal symbol of primordial beginnings: the night-dark potentiality of the egg. In the second case, you may see the oval as an image of the void, a cosmic blank, a dark unreflective mirror into which you look as through a glass darkly. Surrounded by an aura of insubstantial translucency, it is a dark moon in eclipse.

The former reading suggests an extrovert response that maximises the potential in things, and looks to find psychic and emotional pleasure in the given aspects of projected situations. The latter finds darkness a metaphor for loss of pleasure, the dark surface as an impediment to vision. The first is the response of one who sees (at that moment) a glass half-full; the second, that of one who sees (at that moment) a glass half-empty.

PAGE 179

Someone said: 'Our heads are round so that our thoughts can travel in any direction.' Thought rarely travels in a straight line, especially when we are not sure what to think about something, and when it does it often tends to mislead us. 'Things keep going round in my head' is a common expression of undirected thought, or mental or psychic confusion, one or other of which constitutes our common condition for a great deal of the time.

A great central diagonal of red is an energetic and unstable five-sided figure, pointing in two directions at once. Reds and diagonals are both, in their different ways, unstable and dynamic. The 'thought circle' is incomplete and viewed, as an ellipse, from a diagonal

angle. At opposite corners right-angled triangles contain perfect rectangles (in one case a square): these have a certain orthogonal – vertical/horizontal – certainty. It is an enigmatic image.

Are you comforted or discombobulated by this painting? Does it make you uneasy with its stark red band, its corner-to-corner diagonal, and the broken circle with its full-stop dot? This may reflect an uncomfortable awareness that conscious thought is indeed unpredictable and incomplete in its operations; however hard we try, will be diverted and disconcerted by incursions from the uncontrollable unconscious. You may prefer for things to be settled and certain in life. It may be the case, however, that you find the image oddly comforting – it may confirm your feelings that some things may be real and constant (geometry, for one) but that, even so, we simply do not see them always as they (really?) are. You may be discomfited, but you can live with that.

PAGE 180

In this strange and powerful image you may see quite different things (the title gives no clue to its possible subject). In a purely abstract image (1) you discern a number of circles, interpenetrating with geometric connecting lines, within a geometric framework: it may seem simply to be a playful, colourful arrangement of shapes and forms. Or (2) you may see it as a space, somewhat complicated and paradoxical, into which is suspended a swinging lamp, or swinging and turning discs as in an optical experiment. Or (3) you may see a mask-like face, with two great, staring eyes and an oval mouth.

Response (1) suggests a down-to-earth temperament, a mind that believes what its eyes see and is quite free of fancy or fantastic projection. Response (2) is quick to discover spatial possibilities, to find action within an imagined place; it seeks to *make sense* of signs and shapes, and finds a reassuring solidity in a projected world of things not unlike the one we inhabit. Response (3) is disconcerting: the mind finds, in a quick and arbitrary projection, an answer to the eye; it is as if the viewer had looked into a distorting mirror. This is a wilfully fanciful, imaginative reaction of a mind that expects the world to be interactive, to conjure surprises.

You will, at different moments, find all three responses in yourself: this reflects the ever-shifting, unstable quality of the brain-eye axis. Given the rough paint marks and crude execution of the work, you will have known from the first instant that this is a *painting*, a physical object; how extraordinary for the working of the mind to have ignored this obvious datum, and effortlessly to have leapt to such quite different interpretations of the image (and possibly many others)!

HAPPINESS

Research has shown that you can help yourself to be happy. What are the conditions of fulfilment? There has been no better answer than that of the Italian polymath Girolamo Cardano, written in 1501:

'Let us live therefore, cheerfully, although there be no lasting joy in mortal things . . .

But if there is any good thing by which you would adorn this stage of life, we have not

of such been cheated: rest, serenity, modesty, self-restraint, orderliness, change, fun,

entertainment, society, temperance, sleep, food, drink, riding, sailing, walking, keeping

abreast of events, meditation, contemplation, education, piety, marriage, feasting, the

satisfaction of recalling an orderly disposition of the past, cleanliness, water, fire, listening

to music, looking at all about one, talks, stories, history, liberty, continence, little birds,

puppies, cats, consolation of death, and the common flux of time, fate and fortune over

the afflicted and the favoured alike. There is a good hope for things beyond all hope;

good in the exercise of some art in which one is skilled; good in meditating upon the

manifold transmutation of all nature and upon the magnitude of Earth.'

WWW.PSYCHOBOOK.CO.UK

•B•	•b•	•B•	•b•	•B•	•b•	•B•	•b•	•B•	•b•	•B•	•b•
•C•	•c•	•C•	•c•	•C•	•c•	•C•	•c•	•C•	•c•	•C•	•c•
•D•	•d•	•D•	•d•	•D•	•d•	•D•	•d•	•D•	•d•	•D•	•d•
•E•	•e•	•E•	•e•	•E•	•e•	•E•	•e•	•E•	•e•	•E•	•e•
•F•	•f•	•F•	•f•	•F•	•f•	•F•	•f•	•F•	•f•	•F•	•f•
•G•	•g•	•G•	•g•	•G•	•g•	•G•	•g•	•G•	•g•	•G•	•g•
•H•	•h•	•H•	•h•	•H•	•h•	•H•	•h•	•H•	•h•	•H•	•h•
•J•	•j•	•J•	•j•	•J•	•j•	•J•	•j•	•J•	•j•	•J•	•j•
•K•	•k•	•K•	•k•	•K•	•k•	•K•	•k•	•K•	•k•	•K•	•k•
•L•	•l•	•L•	•l•	•L•	•l•	•L•	•l•	•L•	•l•	•L•	•l•
•M•	•m•	•M•	•m•	•M•	•m•	•M•	•m•	•M•	•m•	•M•	•m•
•N•	•n•	•N•	•n•	•N•	•n•	•N•	•n•	•N•	•n•	•N•	•n•
•P•	•p•	•P•	•p•	•P•	•p•	•P•	•p•	•P•	•p•	•P•	•p•
•Q•	•q•	•Q•	•q•	•Q•	•q•	•Q•	•q•	•Q•	•q•	•Q•	•q•
•R•	•r•	•R•	•r•	•R•	•r•	•R•	•r•	•R•	•r•	•R•	•r•
•S•	•s•	•S•	•s•	•S•	•s•	•S•	•s•	•S•	•s•	•S•	•s•
•T•	•t•	•T•	•t•	•T•	•t•	•T•	•t•	•T•	•t•	•T•	•t•
•U•	•u•	•U•	•u•	•U•	•u•	•U•	•u•	•U•	•u•	•U•	•u•
•V•	•v•	•V•	•v•	•V•	•v•	•V•	•v•	•V•	•v•	•V•	•v•
•W•	•w•	•W•	•w•	•W•	•w•	•W•	•w•	•W•	•w•	•W•	•w•
•X•	•x•	•X•	•x•	•X•	•x•	•X•	•x•	•X•	•x•	•X•	•x•
•Y•	•y•	•Y•	•y•	•Y•	•y•	•Y•	•y•	•Y•	•y•	•Y•	•y•
•Z•	•z•	•Z•	•z•	•Z•	•z•	•Z•	•z•	•Z•	•z•	•Z•	•z•
•a•	•A•	•a•	•A•	•a•	•A•	•a•	•A•	•a•	•A•	•a•	•A•
•b•	•B•	•b•	•B•	•b•	•B•	•b•	•B•	•b•	•B•	•b•	•B•
•c•	•C•	•c•	•C•	•c•	•C•	•c•	•C•	•c•	•C•	•c•	•C•
•d•	•D•	•d•	•D•	•d•	•D•	•d•	•D•	•d•	•D•	•d•	•D•
•e•	•E•	•e•	•E•	•e•	•E•	•e•	•E•	•e•	•E•	•e•	•E•
•f•	•F•	•f•	•F•	•f•	•F•	•f•	•F•	•f•	•F•	•f•	•F•
•g•	•G•	•g•	•G•	•g•	•G•	•g•	•G•	•g•	•G•	•g•	•G•
•h•	•H•	•h•	•H•	•h•	•H•	•h•	•H•	•h•	•H•	•h•	•H•
•j•	•J•	•j•	•J•	•j•	•J•	•j•	•J•	•j•	•J•	•j•	•J•
•k•	•K•	•k•	•K•	•k•	•K•	•k•	•K•	•k•	•K•	•k•	•K•
•l•	•L•	•l•	•L•	•l•	•L•	•l•	•L•	•l•	•L•	•l•	•L•
•m•	•M•	•m•	•M•	•m•	•M•	•m•	•M•	•m•	•M•	•m•	•M•
•n•	•N•	•n•	•N•	•n•	•N•	•n•	•N•	•n•	•N•	•n•	•N•
•p•	•P•	•p•	•P•	•p•	•P•	•p•	•P•	•p•	•P•	•p•	•P•